PRAISE FOR *LEA*

'This book does what it says on the cover. Thanks to *Lead Beyond The Edge*, you really connect with Frederique's mission to help people, one brain at a time, AND you accomplish your own extraordinary. She lives her extraordinary, and she shows you how you can too: this book shows you the way, step by step. This is a must!'

Hal Elrod, international keynote speaker and bestselling author of *The Miracle Morning* and *The Miracle Equation*

'Change happens. Things and people change. They always have and always will. Change is what drives life, and *Lead Beyond The Edge* is an easy-to-read book that helps you embrace change. Frederique's unique experiential approach successfully nudges us gently out of our comfort zone and her subtle scientific strategies for the mind accompany us along the bold path that leads to the edge and beyond. This is a must-read for any leader, for anyone, who is looking to create sustained change at work and at home.'

Elmar Mock, serial inventor and industrial designer, inc. the SWATCH watch, Founder of *Creaholic*

'Rarely does a book come along that actually addresses ALL the areas I think are critical for change, let alone transformation. This book gives you the actual path to actual change – and lets you keep the change!'

Amanda Gore, award-winning keynote speaker, bestselling author in the fields of joy, resilience and leadership, CEO of *The Joy Project*

'*Lead Beyond The Edge* is a must-read book for anyone who wants to succeed. As you read this book, you will find Frederique there with you, authentically, strategically and scientifically guiding you through every step of your journey. Her genuine passion and her expertise shine through as she inspires and empowers you to build success in your own life and in your organization. While the research is impressive and uniquely presented, there is something captivating about how she manages to magically weave her personal stories into the message. What a magnificent book.'

Sean Gallagher, successful entrepreneur, business coach, bestselling author of *Secrets to Success* and former investor on *Dragons' Den* TV Show (*Shark Tank* in the US)

'*Lead Beyond The Edge* is one of the few books out there that makes the science of how we think and act easy to understand and practical to implement. Frederique offers you a clear guide as to how to apply insights from psychology and neuroscience to change your life. It is very well researched and offers a very clear roadmap to success. You will find it immensely useful.'

Owen Fitzpatrick, psychologist and creator of the *Changing Minds* podcast

'If you'd like to know the "why behind the why" on achievement, then you will greatly enjoy *Lead Beyond The Edge* to take your life further than you ever dreamed possible. This book is the most cerebral technical explanation and application of goal-setting I've ever read. Frederique makes it both interesting and informative. Buy this book and lead yourself to extraordinary results!'

Tom Ziglar, author and proud son of Zig Ziglar

'Pay attention to the detailed framework and systematic approach of this book filled with strategies, science, and stories. Enjoy the design and delivery as Frederique becomes your sherpa guiding your journey as you commit to get out of your comfort zone and achieve extraordinary results in your personal and professional life.'

Neen James, attention expert, keynote speaker and author of *Attention Pays*

'No surprise that Frederique has created such a well thought-out, compelling and potent book: she has made it her life's mission to help others ignite their transformational possibilities and achieve goals through shrewd strategies. The clever imagery of Circuits and Wires acts as a clear roadmap, providing the reader with artful moments of science, inspiration and practical solutions. Frederique has combined all her knowledge, skills and personal triumphs into a fascinating journey of discovery and success. Over 20 years of insights condensed into one book so anyone can apply positive psychology, neuroscience and behavioural change to create their own epic story of achievement, and lead beyond the edge.'

Poll Moussoulides, vocal communications and personal performance specialist, Director at *Voice Matters International*

'Frederique Murphy has written a must-read book for anyone looking to be inspired and equipped to achieve success. Her framework is a step-by-step guide with actionable tools rooted in neuroscience. Frederique's writing style is charismatic and engaging which can often be hard to accomplish when marrying science and inspiration. I highly encourage anyone looking to accomplish personal and career goals to read this book.'

Lori Pugh Marcum, Head of Meeting Innovation, *Meeting Professionals International*

'Winning is a state of mind. It is clear that Frederique has not only your mind in mind but also your brain and heart. The book has practical and memorable scientific content, which helps you understand and learn how to control specific aspects of your mind. Her strategies are written to guide you through facing your challenges and help you win in life.'

Paul Boross, *The Pitch Doctor*, keynote speaker, bestselling author, communication expert, Sky TV's *School Of Hard Knocks* team psychologist

LEAD BEYOND THE EDGE

THE BOLD PATH TO EXTRAORDINARY RESULTS

FREDERIQUE MURPHY

First published in Great Britain by Practical Inspiration Publishing, 2021

ISBN 9781788602143 (print)
9781788602136 (epub)
9781788602129 (mobi)

The *Lead Beyond The Edge* framework was designed by Frederique Murphy and illustrated by Andrew Pagram of Beehive Illustration.

DEDICATION

To Roland,
not only an extraordinary leader,
but to me, an extraordinary husband,
whose love helps me to let go of the past,
allowing my future to become my present:
with you in my life, every day is indeed a gift!

CONTENTS

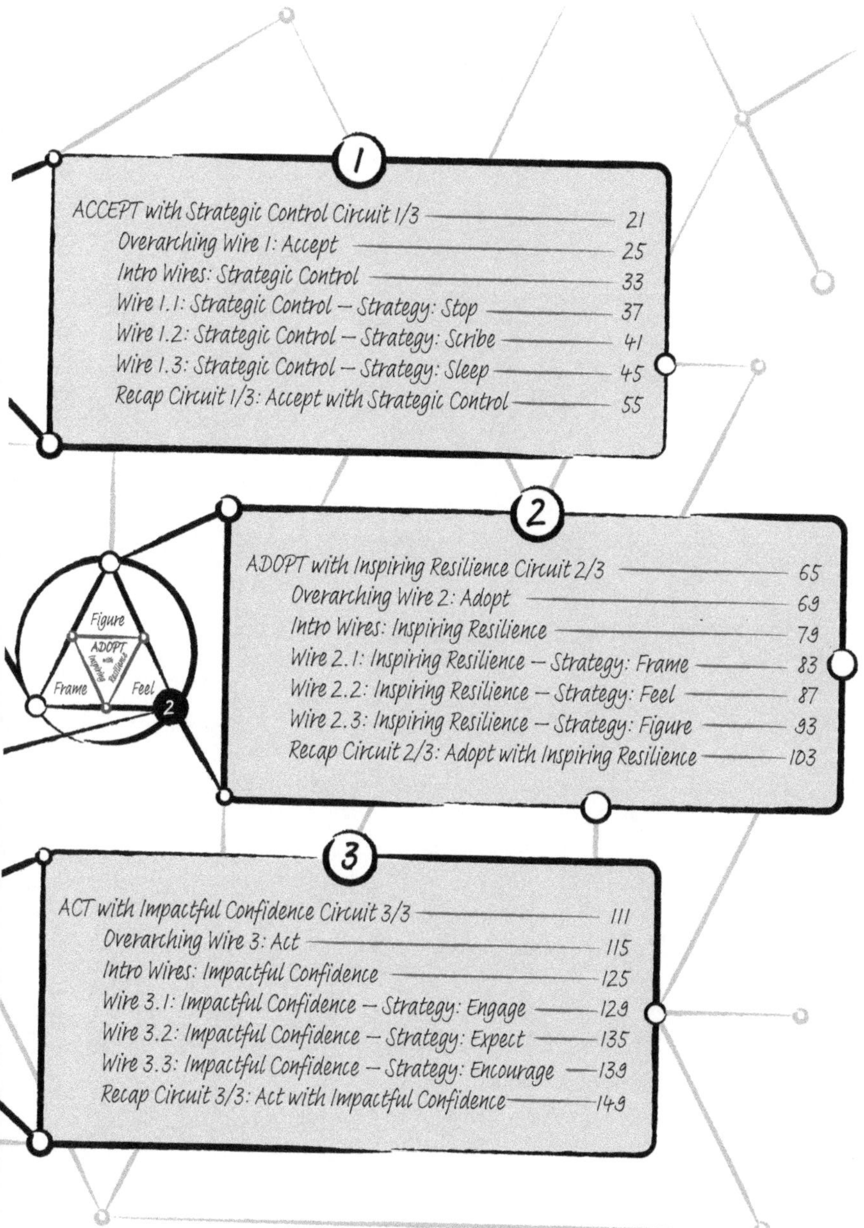
1
2
Figure
ADOPT with Inspiring Resilience
Frame
Feel
2
3

LIST OF ILLUSTRATIONS

FOREWORD

'*The greatest discovery of my generation is that human beings can alter their lives by altering their attitudes of mind.*' These words are often attributed to William James, famed philosopher and psychologist, known by many as the founder of American psychology, although – as is often the case with quotes attributed to intuitively likely sources – there's no indication that Dr James ever actually said it.

But whomever we have to thank for this quote, I believe it is true, fantastic and absolutely game-changing! Think about it: it means that while you cannot control everything, or even the majority of things, that occur in your professional and personal life, you can ultimately and absolutely control your success – this is you leading your life. And that is big!

Still, when it comes to altering your life, simply wanting to is not enough. The desire to change is important, of course: it is the start of your success path. But without a guide it can be enormously difficult to advance far enough on your journey to really change the game.

This is where my treasured friend and colleague Frederique Murphy comes in. She does so via this superb book that you are either checking out online or at the bookstore, or that you already have in your hands and from which you are getting ready to greatly benefit. This is authentic and powerful teaching from one of today's great thinkers and leaders, guaranteed to help you learn, think and lead – whether leading yourself or others within your organization.

I first met Frederique (aka @IrishSmiley) on Twitter. At least I think that's where I first met her. You know how when you become great friends with someone you eventually might forget where or how you even met? You just know you deeply admire and respect that person and it might even feel as though you've always known them.

The moniker @IrishSmiley definitely suits her (even though she is actually half Irish/half French: as she often states, her accent is French, but her heart very Irish!), as she brings her wonderful smile to every conversation, whether in person or online, one-to-one or in front of thousands of people from stage at one of the numerous international corporate events at which she often speaks. She simply IS that person.

Frederique's leadership and spirit shine right through. What most people don't know is that the hurdles she overcame and the immense personal and professional transformation she achieved were the result of the very knowledge and wisdom she so generously shares with us in this book.

So since you can alter your life by altering your attitudes of mind, now we must ask: 'Is there a methodology – a system, if you will – that can actually do for you what it did for Frederique?'

And fortunately, the answer is yes. Know this: regardless of where you are now, regardless of your personal fears, regardless of any internal, mind-based limitations you feel you have, you can actually change your life for the better by learning how to alter your mind.

Lead Beyond The Edge shows you exactly how to do that, step by step, from belief to attitude to behaviour, providing you with actionable strategies to overcome any challenges as you progress from 'I want to do it!' to 'I did it!!!' as you successfully achieve your goals.

In leadership, there is strength in authenticity, and Frederique leads you on this bold path by sharing her personal stories with you. Through these intimate narratives, you'll come to know her and know that she is there for you as your guide on this journey. Her instruction, however, is far from anecdotal.

The framework for success you are about to learn is fully backed up by science, which Frederique demystifies for you in her unique and clear way, so that it is understandable and accessible. As you'll see, she diligently shares with you the neuroscientific or psychological insights behind every strategy in this book: it is solid, well researched, and memorable, and most importantly it works.

The result is that your life, at work and at home, will never be the same. You will use the power of your mind and actually rewire your brain. This is what makes this book game-changing. Frederique provides you with the keys to your mind and your brain. I don't know about you, but to me that is very, very exciting! It means that your happiness, your wellbeing and your success are absolutely within your control.

So I now introduce to you one of my favourite people, Frederique Murphy, and invite you to welcome her and let her guide you to push through your comfort zone to lead beyond the edge and achieve your own extraordinary results.

Wishing you stratospheric success!

Bob Burg, Co-author of *The Go-Giver* and *The Go-Giver* book series

ACKNOWLEDGEMENTS

Sitting down to write this section, I'm so full of joy and beaming with gratitude. As you'll soon discover from reading and experiencing this book, I've poured my heart and brain into *Lead Beyond The Edge*. And a lot of love too, in every part of this book project.

Every single interaction and event in my life has helped me bring this book to fruition for you to lead beyond the edge. At a time when the external narrative is so strong all around us, I'm grateful for everything and everyone around me. You are holding this book in your hands thanks to these extraordinary people.

Thank YOU

My publisher: *Practical Inspiration Publishing*. Alison Jones and her team, Shell Cooper, Michelle Charman, Judith Wise. Alison, you were one of the very first people to see the potential in my idea and, like they say, the rest is history. I believe in this book so much and it has been a pleasure working with you and your team. This was a real partnership, and I thank you.

My project manager, Lizzie Evans at *Newgen Publishing UK*. Lizzie, you have been there at every stage of the book production process, from cover design, to copy-editing, typesetting and proof-reading, and you have been phenomenal. I appreciate your guidance, knowledge, patience working with me and my meticulousness, drive and desire to produce the best book possible, and I thank you.

My beta readers: Amy Brann, Aoibhe Cantwell, Owen Fitzpatrick, Katie Lernihan, Noreen McGuire, Roland Krijnen. Each of you, in your own individual and expert way, has helped me make this book stronger. From getting your 'Yes, I'm doing it!' to receiving your superb feedback, your valuable input has meant the world to me, and I thank you. **My development editor, Kate Llewellyn.** You gave me incredible insights and notes on my beta draft and, along with my beta readers' feedback, these have helped me take the book to another level, and I thank you.

My copy-editor, Susan Jarvis. Sue, it was beautiful to work with you together, making the manuscript better while preserving my voice, and I thank you. **My proofreader, Joanna Pyke.** How wonderful to have you review the first proofs to help me fine-tune it all ensuring the content was free of errors, and I thank you.

My book cover designer, Fiachra McCarthy. You listened to my brief and designed a cover that gives me goosebumps every time I see it. I'm counting the days till I see it on the shelves and hold it in my hands for the very first time. You created something outstanding, and I thank you. **My illustrator, Andrew Pagram of *Beehive Illustration*.** You brought my framework to life with your illustrations, adding that extra touch I wanted for my readers' experience, and I thank you.

My speakers and authors peers, mentors, family and friends. You are there for me and *you* know who you are. You inspire me, challenge me, support me, and I thank you.

My clients. As you know, I am here for you to enthuse you to act towards your dreams, stretch you beyond what you think you can be, do and have, inspire you to be the best that you can be, believe in you in those times you've temporarily stopped and guide you along your M3 journey. I idolize people who lead beyond the edge. It is special to me to witness you push through your fears and make it happen, and for that, every single one of you is one of my idols, and I thank you.

My special places. My attendees often comment that I look at home on stage, and it is true I feel at home on stage delivering my keynotes for my clients. **Stage** is my second home. My first one is **my husband's arms.** And I do have a third one: **Ashford Castle.** What makes this place magical is the people, and the reason why it is so important to me and this book. I actually came up with the *Lead Beyond The Edge* title there during a brainstorming session in the Drawing Room, and last year, I signed my publishing contract in one of their suites. Thank you to the excellent team for always making me feel special.

Maman. Thank you for giving me the gift of life and teaching me the values I hold so very close to my heart. **Sébastien, Fabien, Ludovic, Loïc.** No matter what, you 4 always have a place in my heart.

Roland. My life started blossoming when I met you, and this book, like many of the projects we've embarked on together over the last 20 years, started with you by my side, every step of the way. Thank you, I could not have done it without you. ILYWMTYBWLTT +1

And, last but not least, **you, my reader**. I thank you for having picked up this book, having invested in yourself, making the decision to make it happen, and as you and I are about to embark on a journey together, I cannot wait, so…

Let's do it and lead beyond the edge!

INTRODUCTION

'Frederique, you are stupid.' 'Frederique, you are fat.'
'Frederique, you are ugly.' 'Not good enough, Frederique.'
'Not going to amount to much, are you, Frederique?'

This *was* my reality. And yet, even in those dark days, I was still dreaming. I dreamed of being someone making a difference in the world. I dreamed of achieving extraordinary results. Being happy. Being healthy. Being in a fulfilling relationship with a loving partner. Being surrounded by great friends. Living in a dream home. Exploring the world. Visiting amazing places. Going on thrilling adventures. Doing what I love most at work. And laughing – laughing out loud.

One day, I caught myself thinking, *'Frederique, what if all of this could happen?'* The words 'what if' were ringing in my ears. What if…? This was a clear shift; I remember how bright it felt too, like turning on all of the lights, being fired up and snapping my fingers as a powerful gesture, a gesture symbolizing the significance of that moment: 'SNAP! YES, I can make things happen!'

That was the moment when I committed to and took responsibility for my beliefs, attitudes and behaviours, and started achieving extraordinary results. Taking responsibility for your life is one of the greatest mindset shifts you'll ever experience for your success. And learning the skills to ensure your beliefs, attitudes and behaviours are aligned and supportive of your goals is the greatest journey of all.

From that moment on, everything I did led me to develop the *Lead Beyond The Edge* framework, which you've already discovered thanks to my non-traditional table of contents! This changed my life so drastically that there and then I knew I wanted to learn as much as I could, so that in turn I could teach others like you to create lasting change too.

And, this is where YOU come in.

This is for you.

This book is for you to **lead beyond the edge**.

I hear you ask: *'Frederique, what is this edge?'* I'm talking about the edge of your comfort zone: everything you want to be, everything you want to have, everything you want to do but aren't yet, don't have yet and haven't done yet are outside of your comfort zone. This book is designed to enable you to lead beyond the edge of your comfort zone, accomplishing your extraordinary: anything, anytime, anywhere.

Being an inspired and equipped leader will impact you in extraordinary ways. It will help you lead powerful practical transformations – and not just for yourself: your colleagues, your teams, your organization will all feel the impact. It is about optimizing your inner power to maximize your results.

EVERYTHING starts in the mind, and I'd like to help you understand and work with yours, not against it, so that everything you want to be, everything you want to have and everything you want to do is within your reach.

Revolutionizing YOUR Success Path!

From my first consciously reached goal, I was hooked, and I knew that having reached one, my next one was on the way. And it sure was! One goal after another after another. And continuing to this day! Ever since that moment, 20 years ago as I write this introduction for you, I've been fascinated by the science of goal achievement.

I continued thinking: what if I could come up with a systematic approach helping you get out of your own way while taking into account the various challenges that arise depending on where you are on your goal journey, thus guiding you throughout the whole span of achievement?

What if we could leverage the power of our minds to wire and rewire our brains for success, and use our amazing brains to map out that path, so that every time we do it, it becomes easier and stronger? Those 2 words, 'what if,' opened up my mind, fired up my brain, and here we are: there is a way, and you are holding it in your hands now.

This book will teach you how to build the required success path to achieve your goals by providing you with the solutions to the problems leaders like you usually encounter along the way. By applying the solid and scientifically based step-by-step framework, you will learn how to create a series of powerful neural pathways to allow your brain to fire up at your command!

You see, I believe in leading by example, and when I launched my 'Mountain Moving Mindset' business, my award-winning speaking, training and consulting company, I wanted not only to talk the talk but also, even more importantly, to walk the walk, helping organizations reap the benefits of tapping into the power of their leaders' minds. I believe there is an incredible strength that comes from learning from someone who has gone through challenges, and subsequently pushed through and made it happen.

You may be thinking that you've already bought and read books about goals, right? I have too, and there are some great books out there covering parts of the goal journey, but from my knowledge of how the brain works, I can tell you that learning chunks here and there is not the most effective way to get the results you want.

Your brain needs to tick boxes along all the parts of your goal journey, to actually lead you to success. One of my missions for you with this book is to provide you with a clear, practical and memorable framework that spans the whole goal journey, taking you from the 'I want to do it' stage to the 'I DID IT!!!' stage.

This is about revolutionizing the success path. You know that common saying: 'Success isn't a straight line'? It is often accompanied by 2 sketches – the one at the top where you have 'what people think it looks like', which is shown as one straight line, then the one at the bottom with a series of up-and-down lines, often looking like a jumbled mess, saying 'what it really looks like'.

I disagree, and refuse to believe that: I want to offer you a different success option. How about a shift in perspective? Success absolutely does not have to look like a jumbled mess. To succeed is to lead beyond the edge, and I invite you to join me and together step onto a very structured path to success, a path hitting a set series of points along the way to support you with whatever comes up, the path to extraordinary results.

I don't use these words lightly, and I even put them on the cover! I'm passionate about your success. I cannot think of anything more special than seeing someone shift: that moment, when their eyes sparkle, their tone of voice changes, their cheeks get rosier because they suddenly believe that they can make it happen – whatever their 'it' is – and then do it, overcoming any challenges that arise, is why I do what I do. This fuel drives me. Every time this moment happens, I know they are now leading beyond the edge.

But doing so requires inner strength to step up. Wherever you are at, there is always that next level to step onto. And that step always requires a shift in our mindset; breaking through to that higher level involves breaking through fears and insecurities, challenges and doubts that come up at those moments. I call this 'the edge.' The edge can be scary, and that fear can keep you from achieving your full potential.

Lead Beyond The Edge is my solution for you, inspiring and equipping leaders like you to lead extraordinarily at work and at home. This distinctive scientific leadership framework gives you the mind strategies you need to act in spite of fear, to inspire and drive change – to lead beyond your edge, again and again and again.

Leadership is, and will always be, a hot topic. But it is often addressed in a frustrating way. You are presented with a ton of research: reports and surveys on the challenges faced by leaders like you in organizations, as well as the best leadership traits for success you should be developing, but there is a gap. Saying that such and such traits are the ones successful leaders must demonstrate becomes a high-level overview checklist and leaves the leader frustrated not knowing how to make it happen.

This book does that by going beyond: it provides you with the teaching to understand how your mind works and neurologically change your brain, so that you can learn not only how to overcome these challenges but also how to develop these best leadership traits. Learning how to lead beyond the edge will result in you leading yourself, your team, your organization with strategic control, inspiring resilience and impactful confidence.

Why Me?

Openness and transparency have always been vital to me, and I feel that this introduction would not be complete without me sharing with you the why behind my career work, and this book – what started all of it.

Growing up, I was hurt by a lot by people around me: hurt by their words, hurt by their opinions, hurt by their actions, and that hurt almost broke me. I say almost because I'm writing this to you now 20 years later, and no, it did not break me; instead, it ignited my passion for human behaviour, wanting to understand what makes people tick.

This first led me to earning a Bachelor's degree with a double major in Communications and Social Psychology, to then studying the scientific fields of Positive Psychology, Neuroscience and Behaviour Change. I pursue all of these mind and brain components and sciences to continuously learn, as much as I can, to expand my expertise in order to help leaders like you drive powerful transformations and make change happen. I'm driven by results.

As I've shared, I've always been fascinated by goals, specifically goal reaching, again and again and again. What happens when we start thinking of a goal? What happens when we start going for it? What happens when something occurs along the way? What can stop us in our tracks? What can make us resist and give up? Etc, etc, and etc.

Everything has been poured into my passion: the power of the mind to rewire the brain for success. This framework was born from 2 decades of studies and insights, of understanding how people work, of working with people in corporate change and business transformation, of dedication to empowering people to make it happen. Two decades of experience have been amalgamated to bring this framework to fruition.

I'm excited because I've written this book for you. And I'm thrilled that you've made the decision to invest in yourself by purchasing it. This is the result of my career work. On stage, I've already had the pleasure and honour to deliver my 'Lead Beyond The Edge' keynote to tens of thousands of professionals around the globe from Dublin to Vancouver to Mexico to Amsterdam to Madrid to Dallas; now, off stage, you can access it too thanks to this book.

Making the Most of It!

This book is divided into 5 parts and their chapters that, in order to support the science behind the framework, I've decided to name as circuits and wires, since as soon as you start on your path, you'll be building, strengthening and activating new circuits and wires in your brain. This is why I'm using the word 'bold' in the book subtitle. Yes, it is a bold, and scientifically proven, solution to teach you how to push through your comfort zone, to lead beyond the edge, and thus to lead yourself towards extraordinary results in your professional and personal life.

You, using your innate malleable brain, are about to learn how to build a new brain circuitry – 1 path, 3 circuits and 12 wires. These are brand new and do not relate to any existing neural circuits. I've created this entire path, along with its 'circuits' and 'wires', for you to build your *Lead Beyond The Edge* path, so that you too can accomplish your extraordinary.

To get the most out of this book, I first recommend reading it cover to cover, so you can build the full path, with its circuits and wires, in your brain; then, as you continue to achieve goal after goal, come back to specific sections as needed. You'll have already seen that to make it as convenient as possible, the table of contents is a graphic representation of the framework, so that you can easily see where you are at and where you are going, enabling you to directly flip through to a specific circuit or wire you need to revisit in light of what you are facing at any point in time.

- The *Launch Circuit* provides you with the foundations behind the framework, from laying out **the problem** to presenting you with **the solution**, as well as covering the science of your brain and its amazing ability to change, wire and rewire itself, so that you discover how you are going to alter your brain. Plus, as this is more than just reading, it is an immersive experience as you physically alter your brain, this circuit also covers the **multisensory learning boosts** I've created for you: these are an integral part of the solution as they intensify your experience and help you retain the information better.
- *Circuits 1, 2 and 3* take you through the 12-step action framework. This is where you can find all the strategies and their science, so that when your brain tries to stop you and says 'no', your mind will know what to do to conquer the challenges, move forward and make it happen.
    - The *Accept with Strategic Control Circuit* focuses on the belief part of the goal journey, introducing you to the first move to leading beyond the edge, and the actionable strategies for you to learn how to control your inner dialogue.
    - The *Adopt with Inspiring Resilience Circuit* focuses on the attitude part of the goal journey, introducing you to the second move to leading beyond the edge, and the actionable strategies for you to learn how to overcome adversity.

- The *Act with Impactful Confidence Circuit* focuses on the behaviour part of the goal journey, introducing you to the third move to leading beyond the edge, and the actionable strategies for you to learn how to stop procrastination.

And last but not least:

- The *Recap Circuit* provides you with the full *Lead Beyond The Edge* framework along with an executive summary, the *Lead Beyond The Edge* manifesto and information about how to access a series of resources to further enhance your journey as you make the extraordinary happen.

Discovering the Book Approach!

My approach when delivering solutions to my clients is experiential as opposed to academic – on stage, this is one of the things that makes me stand out: my ability to translate complex scientific research and concepts, whether neuroscientific or psychological ones, into useable chunks for my audiences to apply. So it will come as no surprise that I'm using that approach in this book too.

This means that you will not find endless footnotes distracting you from the practical and results-driven content; instead, should you want to, you will find in the References section a non-exhaustive list of the books and the scientific studies and papers behind the effectiveness of the strategies. So, if you want to make the time to dive in, then you can, but if not, rest assured that I've done the work and studied and distilled it all down for you, so you can easily absorb it.

Each of the wires covers **the strategy**, describing how to apply it as the solution to the challenge that you are facing, as well as **the science** that underpins it – provided in a non-academic and digestible way. And to deepen your learning and your experience, **the story**: connecting with you ensures that your brain is fully engaged, and an engaged brain learns better.

I love using storytelling from stage and with my consulting and coaching clients, and I want to do this with you too, so as a reader you will also benefit from the impact of telling stories on the brain. Thanks to scientific research, we know that stories have the ability to shape our brain by changing our beliefs, attitudes and behaviours. When we listen to stories, our brain becomes more active, activating both rational and emotional parts, thus increasing our engagement.

Plus, you'll soon discover that I am using a specific storytelling technique, called story loops, where I layer a series of stories within each other, opening and closing them throughout the flow of the book. Not only does this help your brain engage and hold attention; it also intensifies the journey you and I are about to embark on together by building anticipation and curiosity – I do love a good dose of suspense, particularly when it is used to maximize your learning!

Let's do it, and lead beyond the edge right now.

Ready?

PROLOGUE

Story 

'Leaving everything behind...'

This had unfolded so fast that I hardly had any time to catch my breath. But thank goodness I did not. Had I thought about this too much, I might not have been here at the boarding gate. This was surreal: 4 days ago, I did not even know I'd be here today, getting ready to board a flight from Nantes, France to Dublin, Ireland. I had secured a 2-month contract at a large American IT organization: at 18, I had just finished high-school and received my Baccalauréat diploma. My next expected step was to go to university.

But right now, I was on my way to the country of my ancestors for a summer job. Ireland had always been close to my heart as it was special to my grandfather. As a little girl, I remember how he would call me to the hallway and have me look up at our family crest. He would tell me how proud he was that we were Murphys and explain to me the importance of our surname motto: 'Fortis es hospitalis', *which means 'Brave and hospitable'. Oh, how much I miss him and our chats.*

This was a challenging flight, although I felt numb for most of it. Every time I'd think back about everything that had happened over the last few years and how things had drastically escalated in the last few months, my eyes would fill with tears. Onboard, surrounded by other passengers, I felt embarrassed and held these back. I felt guilty. 'Could I have done more?' I knew I tried but was so afraid of what would happen to me. I felt ashamed.

My heart ached. It ached A LOT. I felt abandoned, lost and alone. I felt invisible. 'Worthless.' 'Not good enough.' 'A failure.' I had become so used to hearing these words that I believed them. So many thoughts rushing through my head: 'Are you crazy, Frederique?' 'What are you doing?' 'You don't even speak English.' 'This is madness.' 'You can't do that.' I tried to put these thoughts at the back of my mind.

Then there was a shift: beyond the fear and all of the doubts and insecurities, I felt the smallest glimpse of hope and realized that this was my moment. The time to leave everyone and everything I knew behind and start anew.

This was scary but it wasn't like I could change my mind anyway: we were in the air, right above the Celtic Sea!

I wanted to believe, and I wanted this: I had found the job and decided to board the plane, and I was ready to make it work. This felt strong. Stronger than just being ready. I felt committed. The captain gave the announcement to his crew: '10 minutes to landing!' I smiled: Wow, this was it: the start of a journey…

Very much like you and I now, about to embark on this journey together. A journey to extraordinary results, where you can lead beyond the edge on a bold path to an extraordinary career, an extraordinary organization, an extraordinary life.

LAUNCH CIRCUIT

▶ Problem ▶

▶ Solution: What and How ▶

▶ A Special Message From Me To You ▶

Everything you desire, wish for and dream of is outside of your comfort zone; it is time to push the walls. It is time to take the necessary steps beyond your fears to break through your comfort zone and reach your next level. It is time to — you've guessed it — lead beyond the edge.

PROBLEM

I want to start by laying out the problem, and I do realize that this may sound unusual for this book and coming from me. And yet it is the exact right place to start. As John Adams said, *'Every problem is an opportunity in disguise.'* And it is very much how I like to tackle problems in my life. Beyond the meaning of the word 'problem', the connotation you have with it is key to handling these as they come up for you too.

From stage, when I'm delivering a keynote for a client to an audience – and you know this to be true, if we've already had the pleasure to meet at an event – I always end up saying that if the word 'mindset' had an A, it would be for Awareness. I'm a strong believer in the power of awareness: the more aware you are, the better you are at handling what comes up, so you can move forward. Gaining more awareness about something makes that something more tangible, thus increasing its reach and your ability to work on it. Awareness leads to change.

Let's dive in and understand the overall and underlying problem with goals. It is actually a one-word problem: change. When you think of your goals, these are for you to be, have and do something different, which means that this requires a change from you. Twenty years ago when I started working in change management, I met one of my very first mentors, who became a very good friend, and I will always remember what he said to me: *'Frederique, here is the key to great change management; it is the fundamental assumption for us to do a great job at it: people do not like change.'*

This may sound obvious to you now, but for me, within the simplicity of that statement lay the solution to communicating most effectively. Using that as a baseline for my strategic plans and steps, I never looked back. I did later study the science behind this phenomenon, which we will cover in this book, as it provided me with an extra layer of understanding and clarity about what is going on in our minds.

By now, you might be thinking, so that's it – that's the problem? Almost…! I want to fine-tune it a bit more. You see, these days my scientific knowledge gives me assurance that this was indeed the right way of approaching change management, and I certainly saw it in the field every day with the teams, but now I wouldn't say *'People do not like change.'* Instead, I want to be more specific and say: *'Our brains do not like change and, at first, resist it.'*

Now, this is a clearly articulated and communicated problem, one that we are aware of and thus can tackle right here, right now. We're doing this because that problem stands right between you and any of your yet-to-be-accomplished goals.

You've heard of the concept of having a comfort zone, right? It's that zone we have around ourselves, the place where we feel safe and comfortable, hence its name. I know that some schools of thought tell you to forget about the zone, but it is not the right thing to do, as we want to be honest with ourselves and increase our awareness: the more we know, the better we can tackle things. So be fine with it. You have a comfort zone. I have a comfort zone. We all have a comfort zone.

It is something we can work with. Its size is also not set in stone. You have the ability to extend your comfort zone, and you can do so as many times as needed throughout your life. What is also interesting is understanding the way our comfort zone works. I'd like you to imagine yourself in the middle of a box – to get even more engaged, grab a pen and paper, and draw a medium-sized square in the middle of the paper, then draw yourself in the middle of the zone, stickman style if you want.

Got it? Okay, so, this zone represents what is *currently* – and that's the operative word – comfortable to you. In this comfort zone, you have everything that you already are, have and are able to do. You can mark these things with dots or crosses all around yourself within your zone on the paper.

Now, think of your goals. The things you are not yet. The things you don't have yet. The things you haven't done yet. All these things are outside your comfort zone. You can mark these things with dots or crosses, but this time you have to draw them on the paper outside your zone.

In order to get to these, you need to start walking towards the edges of your comfort zone, and as you get closer, the problem kicks in and your brain resists and starts sending you all kinds of 'stuff' – yes, you know what I'm talking about: fears and insecurities, challenges and doubts.

Yes, that type of stuff. Fear lives in the edges of your comfort zone. Every time you aim towards reaching new heights, you'll encounter fear. See it as a door opening up to bigger things and push it!!!

There is this misconception around fear: it is seen as something to avoid. Having studied how the brain works, and being fascinated with growth and development, I have a different point of view on this. In order to equip you with everything you need to be bold and accomplish extraordinary results, we need to stop avoiding fear and instead learn about it, learn from it and understand it.

At this point you have 3 choices. I refer to these as your 3Fs, where F stands for Fear, so that you can easily remember them. These 3Fs are the 3 ways of reacting to having approached that fearful edge:

- Fall back.
- Freeze.
- Fight.

Let's talk about each of these reactions. I know I certainly can relate to each and every one of these reactions on this list.

When you *fall back*, it is like you basically put your hands up, shake your head from left to right, think to yourself, '*Not going to happen*', and decide to go back inside to the middle of your comfort zone. It is the easy path and it happens to all of us. Before I knew what was going on and understood the reason behind all of it, this happened to me too.

When you *fight*, it is like you basically put your hands up, but this time, you form fists with your hands, shake your head from top to bottom, think to yourself, '*Yes, this is happening*', and decide to go outside of your comfort zone. These are the times when you went for it and reached your goals. It may be inconsistent, but I'm sure you can relate to having been there before. Again here I can relate – before I had my framework, I had results, but these were inconsistent too.

I know you are thinking, '*Hey, Frederique, wait a minute, what about the middle option – what happens when we freeze?*' Good question! When you *freeze*, you give your mind the time it needs to conquer your brain's initial fear response, and to choose to *fight* instead. Yes, on one hand you might be thinking, '*I want to fight straight away*', but on the other hand picking the middle option gives you the opportunity to pause and be present, then you can decide what you want to do. This *freeze* option leads you to make an informed decision: *fall back* or *fight* and accomplish your goal.

So, where do we go from here? Well, since everything you desire, wish for and dream of is outside of your comfort zone, it is time to push the walls. It is time to take the necessary steps beyond your fears to break through your comfort zone and reach your next level. It is time to – you've guessed it – lead beyond the edge.

My systematic approach gives you the moves, step by step, that you need to make it happen again and again and again: every time, no matter what comes up for you. Follow these and consistently *fight* – even if you are first making the time to pause and freeze, so you consistently decide to go outside of your comfort zone. It is time to bridge the gap between the fear and the opportunity to change. Your best moments are on the other side of your fears. So, let's do it and access the solution!

SOLUTION: WHAT AND HOW

'I will not follow where the path may lead,
but I will go where there is no path,
and I will leave a trail.' Muriel Strode

The solution comes in 2 parts, which you can think of as 2 sides of the same coin. On one side, I'm going to take you through my framework and on the other side, we are going to leverage your mind. Your mind is the engine behind the framework. Using the power of your mind, we are together going to rewire your brain for success.

Remember what I said in the introduction – the bit about when your brain tries to stop you and says 'no,' your mind will know what to do to overcome the challenges, move forward and make it happen? That's how it is going to work. By systematically providing you with the solutions to the challenges that come up throughout the span of achievement for each and every one of your goals.

The What

First, let's talk about the *what* of the solution: your brain, and to do that we are going to review a few key facts and figures. My objective here isn't to get too scientific; I see no need in drowning you in too much information. Instead, I've carefully picked out the facts and figures I want to share with you, those that will equip you with the necessary knowledge, understanding and anticipation of what's to come as we kick off this journey together.

Once you know – really know – how amazing your brain is, this will open up the extraordinary for you. Your adult brain weighs on average 3 pounds, or 1.5 kilograms, and you can imagine it fitting in the palm of your hand. Its cellular composition is where the power lies. I know, I know, I used the word 'power.' Bear with me, I'm going to show you why I'm using that word: this is truly remarkable.

Your brain has 4 lobes; when I teach neuroscience during my training classes, I always give this handy mnemonic device to my students: 'FTOP'; this acronym stands for Frontal, Temporal, Occipital and Parietal. So now, you can imagine a brain or even draw one on a piece of paper – a simple oval shape will do. Remember, the more engaged you are, the better you are at learning and retaining the information. So, imagine or draw a brain with a stem, and place the brainstem on the right. Got it?

Okay, at the front, on the left, you can imagine or draw a vertical line – that's your frontal lobe. Then divide the rest with a horizontal line, and at the top you have the parietal lobe. At the bottom, divide the remaining space into 2, where the left space is twice as big as the right space, and there you have the temporal lobe on the left and the occipital one on the right.

It is great to know about these lobes, so that when later in the book I talk about such and such part of the brain and mention which lobe it belongs to, you'll be right there with me.

For over half a century, neuroscientists reported that we had approximately 100 billion nerve cells, called neurons, in our brain; a more recent study has determined that this number is closer to 86 billion. Still, a lot of neurons, right? I mean, take a moment here to visualize this: your brain has 86 billion neurons. Such a brain-blowing number, isn't it? But there is more!

These neurons communicate with each other through electrical and chemical signals, an electrochemical process, to make everything happen. Nothing happens unless at least 2 of your neurons talk to each other. There are 3 parts to a neuron: body, axon and dendrites: the axon transmits information away from the cell body – you are going to love the name of this process: we refer to it as an 'action potential', while the dendrites – *dendron* is the Greek word for tree, which is very appropriate, as your dendrites look like tree branches – collect information for the cell body.

Synapses are the junctions between your neurons; they allow messages to pass through the gap from neuron to neuron. And wait until you find out about this number. On one neuron, there are on average 7000 synaptic connections to other neurons. And now you can do the maths to expand your mind even more: 86 billion multiplied by 7000… brain-blowing indeed! No wonder I used the word 'amazing' when introducing your brain to you, right?

The more times a message is transmitted from one neuron to another neuron, the more it makes that synapse stronger and stronger. By repeating activity, you have the power to wire and rewire your brain. You can create a neural path, and then strengthen it, over and over and over again, making it easier and easier to go through that path.

This brings us to discuss neuroplasticity. I know this sounds like a big word, but it does not have to be. Neuroplasticity is the name of the process whereby your brain is plastic and thus has the ability to change. It allows your brain to adapt and evolve. For several decades, scientists thought the brain was static and hard-wired.

Those previous decades of scientific 'certainty' explain why still, to this day, it is one of the most common myths about the brain, but it is one that needs debunking right here and now. We now know this is not true at all. You can alter your brain, rewire existing connections as well as wire new connections, and you can do this throughout your entire life. Yes, even in adulthood. New neural connections are formed during our lifetimes; they do not stop at a particular age despite previous beliefs.

These are important truths, and I will never get tired of presenting them from stage and opening up my audiences' brains. I particularly remember presenting a few years ago in front of a group of high-level executives, where the median age was about 45 to 50. This executive walked up to me at the end and said, '*Thank you Frederique: you've totally changed my reality*.'

He had believed that his brain had stopped changing as an adult and, while he had felt he had reached his career peak, he now knew he had believed and held onto that misconception for too long. From that day onwards, he accepted he could wire and rewire his brain, opening up so many things for himself by igniting new beliefs, attitudes and behaviours. I'm still in touch with him and over the years I've seen him continue to climb the corporate ladder, expanding his work with bigger scope and teams.

Michael Merzenich (2013), a neuroscientist and a pioneer in brain plasticity research, said: '*Your brain – every brain – is a work in progress. It is "plastic". From the day we're born to the day we die, it continuously revises and remodels, improving or slowly declining, as a function of how we use it*.'

There are so many examples of neuroplasticity to share, and I've picked one of my favourites to share with you. The Cochlear implant was co-developed by Michael Merzenich. This device also works in 2 parts. On one side, you have the implant itself and on the other side, your brain.

The implant lets the person hear sound and the brain changes itself, so that it makes the implantation successful – the brain, specifically here the central auditory system, responds to the implant stimuli and generates plastic changes. As a result, it restores hearing and facilitates language in profoundly deaf people. This is one of the many remarkable examples of neuroplasticity, giving us clear evidence that our brain is capable of remodelling and creating new pathways.

Talking about pathways, I must introduce you to Donald Olding Hebb, the father of neural networks. He was a psychologist, specializing in neuropsychology. His last name might be familiar to you if you've heard of Hebb's Rule. This is his most significant contribution to neuroscience and his findings were published in 1949.

The rule is often summed up as: '*Neurons that fire together wire together*'. It is the basis of the brain plasticity, forming and strengthening pathways in our brains. Donald Olding Hebb also talked about repetition and persistent stimulation, which leads me to share with you that neuroplasticity is indeed enhanced by these 2 components. Throughout this book, as I guide you to create your very own path, you will see that I'm using these 2 keys to make sure you make the most of it as you build your circuits and wires.

Emotional intensity simply happens every time you feel strongly; that intense emotion helps provide you with meaning and gives value to the action you are undertaking. Your strongest memories, whether good or bad, are vivid because of their emotional intensities. When you attach powerful feelings to an experience, you engage and enhance the path of that action. The brain change is supported by your commitment and responsibility to make it happen. Your emotions help fire up your neurons as you activate your circuits.

Repetition pretty much speaks for itself: repeat, repeat, repeat and you strengthen your circuits, wires and path. I like to use this analogy on stage. Imagine you are out and about in the countryside and are standing in front of a pristine field of grass – this is A, your starting point. You want to go to the other side – B, your reaching point. At this time, there is no trail yet.

So you start walking on the fresh grass to reach B. Once at B, as you turn around and look back at A, you notice that the grass is not untouched anymore and you can actually see a very fine trail, where you first decided to walk. Now imagine going back to A. You'll follow that very same thin trail back. This time, as you reach A again and look back at B, the fine trail is not as thin anymore, and you can start seeing a path forming. As you continue to walk back and forth a few more times, that path becomes clearer and clearer.

This is neuroplasticity in action: the very same thing happens in your brain as you form new connections, circuits, wires and pathways. This is one of my favourite quotes from Henry David Thoreau: '*A single footstep will not make a path on the earth, so a single thought will not make a pathway in the mind. To make a deep physical path, we walk again and again. To make a deep mental path, we must think over and over the kind of thoughts we wish to dominate our lives*.' How insightful he was, centuries before neuroplasticity was discovered and scientifically proven.

And what a breakthrough discovery it was! Not only does neuroplasticity help with traumas, injuries and strokes, but you can also take charge of this process for your success, which is what you are doing here with me and this book: self-directed neuroplasticity.

Having absorbed the figures and facts I have just shared with you, I know you are now thinking of your brain as amazing and neuroplasticity as remarkable indeed. Changing your brain is possible, proven again and again by scientific research, and entirely up to you to activate. Now you know why I felt so compelled to use such a strong word as 'remarkable.' You have it in you: you can use the power of your mind to wire and rewire your brain. If there was ever a time to use that word, I'm sure you agree with me that this is the time.

This ability of yours is the remarkable key behind the framework. You can make this work for you by trusting your brain to support you with the direction in which you want to lead. It is about you taking control of your brain and making it work as you discover the framework and build your *Lead Beyond The Edge* new brain circuitry, as you form your bold path to extraordinary results.

The How

So, second, now that we have discussed the 'what', let's talk about the 'how' of the solution: the *Lead Beyond The Edge* framework, which consists of 3 circuits, including 4 wires each (one overarching wire and 3 supportive ones) – altogether, the 12 wires you need to build and strengthen the full path.

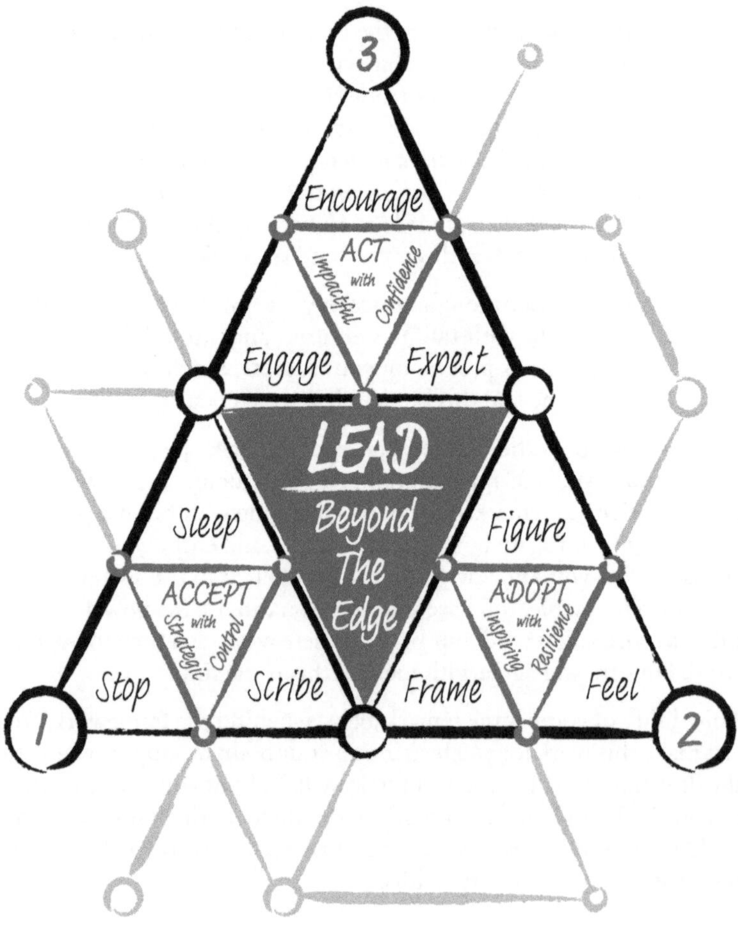

Illustration 1: The *Lead Beyond The Edge* full framework

This is the framework that will take you again and again and again from the exciting 'I want to do it' stage of your goal to the exhilarating

'I DID IT!!!' stage as you achieve it. Throughout this book, we will go through each of the 12 solution steps together, one after the other, so you learn how to tackle any challenges along your way.

Over the years, I've recognized 3 absolute key moments you need to have in alignment in order to achieve any of your goals, and these are the basis of the 3 circuits you are going to build. The first one takes you from 'Can I?' to 'I CAN!'; the second one takes you from 'I CAN!' to 'I CAN-DO it!'; and the third one takes you from 'I CAN-DO it!' to 'I DO it!'

The idea is simple. And yes, I'm standing by simplicity. Something that is simple can very unfortunately often be overlooked or even dismissed – what a pity. Simplicity is incredibly empowering. Knowing or having heard of some of this content does not take anything away from it.

Food comes to mind here. According to my family and friends, I'm a good cook and a great baker – if we are connected on social media, you must have seen some of my *patisseries*! There is nothing better than a simple dish executed perfectly. It is brilliant on the plate and on the palate. You know of eggs, flour, butter, milk, cream and sugar, right? By themselves, these are a handful of simple and ordinary ingredients. And yet, when combined in a very specific way, in a very specific order, for a very specific purpose, it makes a soufflé, and in the oven it creates the extraordinary.

This framework does that by leading you to achieve your goals: anything, anytime, anywhere. When put together, it gives you the bold path to extraordinary results!

The idea is a flow. Think about the first law of motion from Isaac Newton. As part of the 3 physical laws, the first law states that 'objects in motion stay in motion.' Using this law, which is logical, and thinking about our goals, the framework provides you with the solutions to whatever could stop your flow, preventing you from moving forward.

The simple, yet most powerful driver behind the framework is that to go from the 'I want to do it' stage to the 'I DID IT!!!' stage, you must continually and consistently be in the 'I'm doing it' flow. That motion is momentum. And building that momentum propels you forward, step after step. It leads you to success.

I want to add here a very important distinction that we need to talk about, as we are about to embark together on your path to extraordinary results. Being in the 'I'm doing it' flow is VERY different from being in the 'Go, go, go…!' rat race. Wellbeing and self-care are of the utmost importance to me, and to your brain: you'll see that mindfulness is woven in and out throughout this book as my approach is both results-driven and mindful.

You absolutely can – not only do I know it personally, as I'm doing it, but I also see it with my clients as they do it too – make it happen, and build and maintain that momentum without sacrificing your wellbeing. The flow you are after is there to guide you to take a continuous and consistent approach towards your steps in achieving your goals.

To do that, you need the strategies to overcome any of the challenges that come up along the way, so that when your momentum is threatened you will know what to do. This also helps you to keep it simple: at any time throughout your goal achievement journey, ask yourself this question to check in on your progress: **'Am I doing it?'**

If the answer is:

- YES, 'I'm doing it', it means you are activating all the right circuits and your brain knows what to do and where to go, fully supporting you and your goals.
- no, as in you are unable to say 'I'm doing it', it means that something has come up and unless you implement the required strategies in that moment to overcome it, that something will interrupt your flow and you will stop yourself in your tracks, jeopardizing your success.

It is that stopping in your tracks that self-sabotages your goals; in those instants, by the end of this book, you will know what to do and activate strategies to help you continue. This is the fire within that ignites your next move.

Checking in is actually part of my daily ritual for any of my ongoing goals. I know I'm on track when I can proudly say, often under the shower, 'I'm doing it'. When I'm not able to say so, I know that something is up, and I revert to the framework so I can identify what's going on, tackle it and move forward. It is as simple as that: the ability to leverage the strength and power of simplicity and make it happen.

The difference between dreams and goals lies in your commitment. This is how the framework works. Everything starts with you: your commitment to want to accomplish one of your goals and your responsibility to stay accountable. It is up to you to take control of your mind to get the results that you want, and I'm here to show you how.

And now, the only thing you need is to be at the 'I want to do it' stage – you don't need anything else. You certainly do not need to know the how. From that point onwards, I'm your guide and will be with you every step of the way. Systematically follow my framework, build your circuits and wires so that you can activate them whenever you need to, remain in the flow, stay on the path and reach your goals.

I'm excited that you're here reading this book. And I want to give you as much as possible, so you experience the most out of this book, and this requires you to be with me in an engaged way. Until we get to meet face to face at an event and I can see your face as an engaged member of one of my audiences, right now, with miles and miles between us, you are here as one of my readers, and the fact that you are holding this book in your hands already tells me we are aligned and in this together.

Not only do our brains learn better when we are fully engaged, but we also now know the importance of emotional intensity and repetition to support the neuroplasticity you are leading as you are about to start building your circuits and wires. And that is why I've decided to include this next section as an integral part of the solution.

Multisensory Learning Boosts

This isn't *just* about reading... you see, I believe in leading by example, and on stage, I often share stories demonstrating exactly how I do that with my audiences, so here, off stage, still delivering to you as one of my readers, I want to continue this by providing you with more than you would normally expect from reading a book.

This is about an immersive learning experience. Thanks to the advancements in the field of neuroscience and some amazing research and studies, we know that the best learning environments are multisensory. Each of our sensing organs, for our 5 basic senses – sight, hearing, touch, taste and smell – communicates with our brain to help us understand what is around us. Each of these systems stimulates brain functions. So when we engage more than one sense at a time, we stimulate the brain in different ways, thus fostering the best results in our learning.

By using a multisensory learning approach as part of the solution, I'm teaching you how to lead beyond the edge in a way that enhances your cognitive functions, thus maximizing your results. I did say on the book cover that this is 'the bold path to extraordinary results,' and I intend to use everything at my disposal to facilitate this for you.

Reading predominantly engages your sight. So, going beyond that, I'm also including additional multisensory learning layers to support you even more. This multisensory learning approach will also foster your neuroplasticity. Remember when I said that neuroplasticity has 2 special ingredients: repetition and emotional intensity? Well, this is going to intensify our building process too.

With this book, not only will you be learning by reading and seeing, but to further support you as you build your new circuitry, you will also:

- *hear* – engaging your auditory sense by accessing the accompanying audio visualizations I've produced for you
- *feel* – engaging your tactile sense by forming the kinaesthetic anchors I've created for you, and
- *smell* – engaging your olfactory sense by playing along with the instructions I've put together for you.

And as with everything else in this book, the science backs up each and every one of these multisensory learning layers. These techniques are effective, impactful and proven to positively impact your brain. With the help of innovative events teams, I've been using these techniques as a speaker and a trainer for a couple of decades, and I've seen, time and time again, how effective these are in enhancing learning as well as boosting engagement and amplifying experience for my event delegates.

As I write this, imagine my excitement as one of the techniques I've been using in my events rooms for years has officially been backed up by science. I had read previous scientific studies about the power of our olfactory system and at the time thought of the idea of using these earlier findings and expanding upon these for the benefit of my clients. While I knew this was working, as I could see the positive results at my keynotes and trainings, I'm thrilled that there is now a 2020 scientific paper addressing the effectiveness and impact of the technique.

I believe in these multisensory techniques and I'm excited to share these with you every time you see the 'brain/bulb' icon. You will find these additional sensory learning boosts within each of the 3 circuits' recap sections. Do implement these learning boosts, because they will reinforce your self-directed learning as you build your circuits and wires. All of this will help you to lead beyond the edge. This is about learning faster, better and longer.

This is how the solution works: remember, you need both sides of the coin, the framework and the power of your mind, to rewire your brain for success. And then you will lead beyond the edge and achieve extraordinary results.

A SPECIAL MESSAGE FROM ME TO YOU

My Pledge to You

Having read the introduction to this book and as we are here wrapping up the *Launch Circuit*, I'm sure that you now know **how** and **what** makes this framework work. As I teach it to you, step by step, over the next 3 circuits, I want to help you stay as engaged as possible so that you make the most of it as you apply and make it work for you.

Your Pledge to Yourself

So here is the *Lead Beyond The Edge* pledge that I'd like you to fill in as you embark upon your trailblazing journey, transforming beliefs, attitudes and behaviours to create lasting change in your life, at work and at home.

I don't want this book to *just* be a book. And I certainly do not want you to read it without a goal in mind, as it would all just be hypothetical. I want this to make an impact for you now. So, let's be impactful and have you decide on a goal right now. This will make the framework come to life for you by combining both theory and practice.

Not only will this help you practically, as it will help you focus on a goal as you learn each of the strategies, but it will also intensify your experience. As for the repetition factor, build the path, reach your goal and then activate it again for your next goal. To that extent, you will find information about how to access a printable template of the following pledge within the *Recap Circuit*. That way, you can download and print out as many copies as you want.

I, ____

(*state your first name and surname*), am committed and responsible for my success.

I have decided to follow the framework and build my success path, so that I can activate any of its circuits and wires for any of my goals going forward.

For now, this is the goal I'm focusing on: I want to

____

____

____

(*state your goal*). Thanks to the strategies in this book, I have everything I need to be in the flow and can say: 'Yes, I'm doing it' at any point throughout my journey.

This momentum will drive me to reach my goal, when I will then proudly say: 'I DID IT!!!'

Nothing will stop me in my tracks, as I lead beyond the edge and achieve my extraordinary results.

____

(*your signature*)

You are extraordinary: you add the extra to the ordinary, with your beliefs, attitudes and behaviours towards your goals.

May you lead beyond the edge and accomplish extraordinary results!

Frederique

Frederique Murphy

ACCEPT with STRATEGIC CONTROL CIRCUIT 1/3

Accepting where you are

is the key to moving forward

to where you want to go.

This is it!
This is where you start making it all happen.
You have identified your goal and are ready to accomplish it.

You are at the 'I want to do it' stage.

When I think about this stage, I feel the excitement and the anticipation of what's to come. I feel it in my hands and actually, thinking about it, I feel it in my whole body. To me, it feels as if there is not only excitement in the air but there is excitement in my mind; my brain starts firing up and it feels like a wonderful surge of energy. You know that feeling, right?

You can access it too, right now, as you think of your goal and the excitement of its accomplishment. So, now it's your turn: imagine how it is going to feel when you accomplish your goal. You can close your eyes if you wish and be sure to be as descriptive as possible. What does it feel like? What do you see? Hear? Touch? Maybe even smell and taste? Got it? Open your eyes. What a feeling, right?

And then, BANG, something happens: your hands start feeling clammy, your throat feels that little bit drier, your breathing feels restricted... All of this because suddenly you hear yourself think 'Can I really?'

This is where the first circuit comes in as part of your *Lead Beyond The Edge* path: the one where you and I are going to build the series of wires in your brain to create the new neural pathways that are necessary to take you from this 'Can I?' stage to our first success point on your journey as you reach your 'I CAN!' stage.

'When you believe a thing,
believe it all the way, implicitly
and unquestionably.' Walt Disney

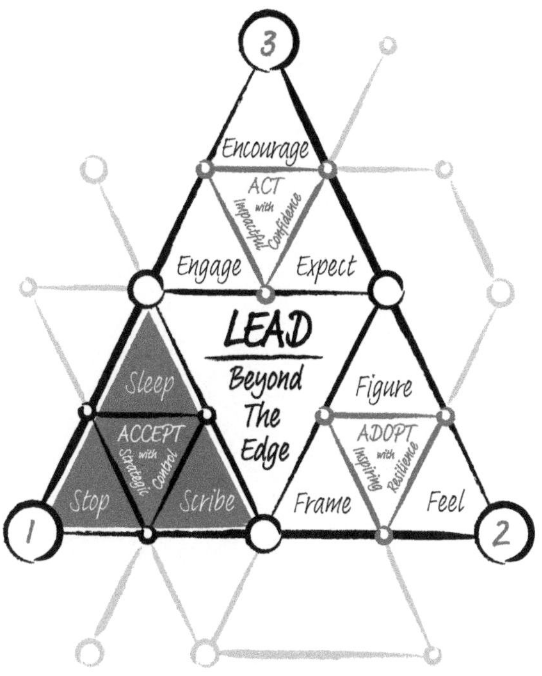

Illustration 2: The *Lead Beyond The Edge* Accept with Strategic Control Circuit framework

This first circuit has everything to do with your beliefs. You will learn how to convince your brain that you can, as well as understand why you have to do this in the first place, expanding your brain knowledge, and you will also know what to do in order to control your inner dialogue so that it stops being destructive.

Remember, the success key leading you to extraordinary results, in an approach that is both results-driven and mindful, is focusing on that 'I'm doing it' flow. Upon building that first circuit and implementing these 3 actionable strategies, there will be no stopping you in your tracks at this stage.

Ready? Let's build it!

From 'Can I?' to 'I CAN!'

OVERARCHING WIRE 1

ACCEPT

Story

'Hiking to an Alaskan glacier…'

I had dreamt about this moment for years, trained for it for months in order to gain the required level of physical fitness, and here I was, in Juneau, Alaska, USA. And, after a strenuous 3-hour trek, I was standing right by the Mendenhall Glacier. The sight was absolutely breathtaking and the air no doubt bitterly cold, though thanks to my 5 different layers of clothes, I could not feel a thing!

We had arrived at the edge of the glacier and before stepping on and exploring the ice, we had paused for a few minutes, and were told to grab our steel microspikes from our backpacks and start strapping them onto our hiking shoes. As all of this was happening, I remember how our guide, Naomi, suddenly went from being cheerful to now having a very stern face and tone.

This. Was. Dangerous. We had signed all of the waiver forms and knew the inherent risks involved in this activity, but there was something about hearing her say we could lose our life on the ice… At that stage, she even gave us the option to stay on the ice while she would go and explore the glacier with the others in our small group. She let us think about this while teaching us how to use the crampons, explaining how these were for ground traction, and the way to safely move onto the glacier was by stomping the icy ground with your feet, short step after short step after short step.

By then, it had hit me: I was terrified and holding on to my trekking poles as tightly as humanly possible and practising how to stomp safely onto the ice, realizing that we were about to head to the glacier over the next few minutes, and the ground was not going to be that flat anymore… The idea that my safety was down to how tightly my feet and crampons would lock onto the ice at various angles during our glacier exploration scared me to my core.

And, internally, I sure felt it. My breathing was out of control, my muscles all tensed up, my heart was pounding, and I even felt the blood drain from my face. I remember thinking: 'Maybe you cannot, Frederique…'

Strategy

As we get started on this journey of achievement, our first circuit is going to be focusing on our beliefs. Everything we want to achieve starts in our brain, ignited and fuelled by our beliefs. So, as we start off this journey, your first mission is going to be to convince yourself that *you can*. It is about developing that unshakeable belief that you really truly believe that you can make it happen. You see, as you are about to embark towards achieving something new, your brain's initial reaction is having none of it. The why behind it is going to make you smile… It is not having any of it yet, because it prefers following an existing path, as it is the easiest path to follow. BUT, and that's a big but, this is where you can take charge and build your ACCEPT circuit, so that you can direct your brain to go up the path YOU lead it to!

This is where we are building the first of the 3 *Lead Beyond The Edge* circuits. As you can see from the highlighted part of this circuit framework in Illustration 3, this is the *Accept with Strategic Control* circuit, and for now we are going to focus on the *Accept* part of it and build that overarching wire on your path.

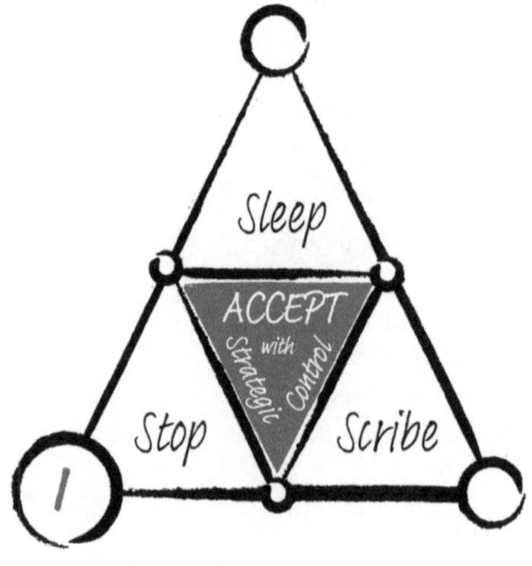

Illustration 3: The *Lead Beyond The Edge* Accept Wire framework

Now, I hear you say, '*Hang on a minute, Frederique... You said, and I agree I could see how this has happened to me in the past, that at this stage my brain goes to panic mode, so how am I supposed to accept that?*'

Accepting where you are is the key to moving forward to where you want to go. And to accept, I'm going to teach you the inner workings of your brain, so you understand why your brain responds in the way it does. I believe that knowledge is power. By demystifying what is going on in that head of yours to have made this panic appear, I am shifting the power to you.

Own where you are: you are about to accomplish something that you've never done before, and your brain is naturally responding to this with panic as this is uncharted territory, and the brain is not finding the path. Take a moment to think about it from the brain's point of view. Your brain wants to be as efficient as possible and you are asking it to go for something that is new; it simply does not know yet how to respond and support you at that moment.

There is this huge misconception out there that successful people – successful executives, successful business owners, successful leaders – do not have fears. This is false. You have fears. I have fears. From what you've already learned in our *Launch Circuit*, you know that we all experience fears. And successful people experience a lot of fears. The difference – and this is the one that makes the difference – is that successful people experience fears AND lead beyond the edge towards success in spite of those fears.

So let's dive in and understand more about how fear starts in your brain. And to do that, we are going to increase your conscious knowledge. This brings me to sharing with you one of my favourite brain quirks – there will be a few more throughout the book, but this one is so astonishing that finding out about it affects everything in the way you think, behave and act. So here I go: you've heard that we have 2 minds, right? A conscious mind and an unconscious mind. Your brain never stops and runs at 100%, so have you ever wondered how much of your neural activity you are actually conscious of?

Most people assume it is a 50/50 split. But this is incorrect. Cognitively, neuroscientists researched this and came up with a more accurate split, where in reality you are conscious of about 5% of your activity, and the rest – 95% – is handled unconsciously. Isn't this amazing? Let that sink in... You are consciously aware of 5% of your neural activity. And this brings us back to the importance of awareness, doesn't it?

Consciously accepting is our first overarching wire on our bold path.

It *is* normal to have fears when you aim at new things, on the way to reaching new heights. And, taking this thinking further, it is up to you to ensure you do not let these fear moments control your beliefs, attitudes and behaviours.

By accepting this, by normalizing it, you are already moving towards a much calmer brain. You are facing your fears by letting your brain know that you understand its initial response.

It is about saying, owning and believing: *'Okay, hang on a minute, I understand and I know what you're doing; I know you and I haven't done it before, and it is normal for you to react like you are right now.'*

It is a new level, like when you are climbing a mountain or going up a steep elevator or being on a plane, and your ears pop: this happens because you've accessed a new level of altitude and this was you simply adjusting to that new level. So now it is about you doing the same here: you are about to accomplish something new, something you've never done before, something that is at a new level of altitude, and you need to accept that to move forward, accept that initially it is entirely normal to receive the new experience with discomfort.

This is about you developing this new belief that will serve you repeatedly as you achieve your goals again and again and again. Beliefs are things we believe to be true and hold onto. Most of our beliefs are initially rooted in our childhood and have since become automatic to us. Our beliefs directly impact our results and success in life, at work and at home.

From positive psychology, we know that there are 2 types of beliefs: on one hand, you can form beliefs that limit you, hold you back from achieving more, prevent you from further growth. These are called *limiting beliefs*. On the other hand, you can form beliefs that empower you, serve and support you on your journey – you've guessed it, these are called *empowering beliefs*.

As an additional level of information and an interesting caveat, I want to say that many of our beliefs are unconscious to us, and they can pop up when these shift from our unconscious to our conscious mind. We have the ability to uncover those beliefs, shift them from limiting to empowering and even form new ones at any time, by rewiring or wiring new neural pathways – which is what we are doing right now with our brand new *Accept* wire within our first circuit.

When I'm working with clients, we often spend time on beliefs during our coaching sessions, as holding on to a limiting belief can be a direct hindrance to our overall success. So using the power of our mind, we become consciously aware of these limiting beliefs and instantly either stop believing in them or shift them to being empowering beliefs to support us with our goals.

Think of your beliefs as if they were a pair of sunglasses… When you put them on, you see the world through their lens. Your beliefs are the lens through which you see the world: they impact your reality. And the type of sunglasses you wear is entirely your choice – like the beliefs you decide to believe in to create your reality. It's 100% up to you, which is exciting as it means you can decide at any time to change, shift and form new beliefs. Paying attention to what you believe in consistently ensures that your beliefs support your aspirations and goals.

Acceptance at that very moment makes you fearless. Being fearless does not mean not having any fears; instead, it means that yes, you are experiencing the fear AND you are persistently and mindfully in the 'I'm doing it' flow. Having grown into acceptance of expecting it and understanding how entirely normal it is for your brain to resist at this stage of the journey, as it is designed to react to the perceived threat, you can then strategically take control of your brain.

This new belief of yours, of accepting the normalcy, gives you the upper hand over your brain as you help it relax. Talking about helping you, let's add the science behind it, as I continue increasing your awareness, and at the same time reinforce this new belief of yours. Once the science is laid out, you'll be fully convinced of how logical it is to react with acceptance.

As absolutely amazing as your brain is, its love of efficiency can lead you along the wrong path sometimes. As mentioned earlier, it is much easier for the brain to lead you along an existing path rather than venturing up a new one – which is where the growth lies.

The easy path is not always the right path; it can be, but not always. While your brain initially fosters the path of least effort, always remember *you are the boss of your brain*, so don't let it get lazy just to reduce effort. Using the power of your mind, you can rewire your brain, and specifically here, create a new wire teaching your brain where you want it to go: this new path is how you lead beyond the edge, and ACCEPT.

Your brain is not afraid of the new thing, your 'it' goal; your brain is initially afraid of the uncertainty of the path, and as it stumbles upon where to go, this uncertainty triggers the *threat response*.

While you might not have heard this scientific term before, physiologically you and I are very familiar with its response: you know those times when your breathing gets impacted, your muscles are tensing up, your heart rate gets erratic… sound familiar? These physiological reactions you are experiencing are the results of your brain having launched its threat response.

I first found out about the threat response in late 2002: I was a change management consultant (yes, I've always been in change!) and in the field I kept noticing these reactions following the expected resistance to the change – this brought me to investigate more (yes, here again I've always been fascinated with the mind and the brain!) as I felt and still fully believe that understanding more about what was going on internally could lead to me putting together the most fulfilling and rewarding strategic plan and steps in order to guide my clients.

You might have read or heard somewhere about the fact that you have an amygdala in your brain, right? We actually have 2. The amygdala is often described as a small, almond-shaped structure, and there is one in each of your left and right temporal lobes. Your amygdalae are involved in your fear and emotional responses, helping you evaluate and process them.

In our endeavour of accomplishing extraordinary results and going for something new, we trigger the threat response because the brain sees this new 'it' as uncertain, and whenever in doubt, in light of uncertainty – whether the threat is real or not – the brain sees it as its duty to protect you and activate this response.

It gets triggered because your brain did not know where to go and in that split-second was unable to direct you, so instead released a hormone called *cortisol*, often referred to as the stress hormone. This is the release that makes you feel out of sorts as it impacts your hands, knees, muscles, cheeks, heart rate, breathing…

At that moment, the brain feels like it was the logical thing to do. Understanding this reaction and raising your awareness eases you into accepting the normalcy of this reaction, thus creating the gap for growth. So, let's back it up and remember what started it, which was you deciding to go for your goal. Because this is something you've never done before, your brain did not know how to guide you.

This is where your amygdalae come in. Your brain, wanting to be as efficient as possible, goes to the amygdalae first to check how it should respond; your amygdalae have been recording your responses since you were born – actually even before that, as we scientifically know that these structures develop at an early embryonic stage. And for our step on this achievement journey, since your goal is new, the amygdalae do not know how to respond as they are not finding anything to support previous responses.

Now you know that, you agree with me, right? It makes absolute sense for your brain to perceive a threat due to the uncertainty trigger, and wanting to protect you, it launches the threat response.

When I'm partnering with a client and delivering a keynote on stage for their audience, I like to use the metaphor of a bookmark. You know, this super handy feature, whereby you can bookmark a specific page on the web...? I mean, we've all been there, right? We are browsing online and after some time, we finally find the exact page that we had been looking for, and this might have taken us 5 to 20 minutes to identify. So logically, to make it easier on us, and more efficient, we use the bookmark feature of our browser, so that next time, next week, next month, next quarter, instead of taking us 5 to 20 minutes to find that page again, it will take us less than a minute as the page will be listed in our bookmarks list, so we know exactly where to go to find it again and again and again. This strategy saves us time and gives us control.

And it's exactly the same for your brain. No bookmark means that a threat is being perceived, and you will feel those physiological reactions in your body. Without our newly built *Accept* circuit, these reactions often lead you to contract and fall back.

But that's not you now, right? You know better than letting your brain stop you in your tracks; now you know that this is happening because of a missing bookmark, and that is it. That awareness brings you more control, which eases you into acceptance, and that acceptance helps you to instantly counteract the effects of the threat response.

This is where you are ready to say:

'I absolutely understand the importance of acceptance, and I accept. By accepting, I'm helping my brain relax into the situation. I understand this is all normal. I understand my fear is normal, since I've not done "it" yet, AND I'm excited for the next step bringing me closer to my goal.'

This new belief that you have formed is a strategic belief, which will support you again and again and again on your way to extraordinary results as you lead beyond the edge.

INTRO WIRES

STRATEGIC CONTROL

You have now set the stage – I love this quote from William Shakespeare: *'All the world's a stage',* as this is what we are doing here together as I guide you to lead yourself in the world.

You have prepared the grounds of your mind by building the overarching *Accept* wire of the first *Lead Beyond The Edge* circuit, using your brain's ability to change and create new pathways. This is the first wire, which with repetition you will strengthen more and more. (Remember the path in the grass analogy I shared with you in the Solution?)

For now, it is time to support you even further by focusing on the second part of the full circuit name: *Accept* **with Strategic Control**. You've already done the work for the *Accept* part and now we continue our path on this journey of achievement by forming the *Strategic Control* wires, thus learning how to control your inner dialogue.

I decided to name this part of the circuit 'Strategic Control' as we live in a world where some things – and sometimes, it might feel, a lot of things – are out of our control. I believe that Strategic Control is a key leadership success trait. It helps us accept that there are things that we do not control: the weather, natural disasters, traffic on your way to work, the way your co-workers think and what they do…

We've talked about the power behind acceptance and here it unfolds again. Trying to change, and often complaining about, things that we do not control leads us to unnecessary and frustrating disappointment. This also ties back to our mindfulness element. The key to our fulfilment and wellbeing is to focus on what we *can* control: our minds. This shift in focus is strategic; it is where you strategically decide to let go of the things that you cannot control and instead take the lead on what you can control.

Remember how I said that this framework is about providing you with all the strategies you need as challenges arise? This is exactly what we are doing here. I'm going to equip you with 3 actionable strategies as you build these 3 new wires so that you can activate these whenever you need them. This is a challenge faced by many, who don't know they have it in them to strategically control it by understanding what's going on in their heads. They aren't holding this book in their hands, though, learning how to be the boss of their brain. *You* are.

Over the years, both with myself and with my clients, I've encountered this challenge more times that I can count. It comes up as we are going for our new goal; it is one of the ways our brain tries to resist. As the path of least resistance, it is easier for it to have you stay in the middle of your comfort zone, and when approaching the edge it fires it up to destabilize and deter you from pushing through. BUT you now know better, and are learning right now how to lead beyond the edge: this is where you can take charge and build your STRATEGIC CONTROL wires, so that you can direct your brain to go up the path YOU lead it to!

Story

Once upon a time

'Preparing for a job interview...'

Sitting on a high stool at the kitchen worktop, I'm trying to concentrate. It is getting late and I'm tired. I'm taking one last look at my preparation notes, browsing through the prospective company website one more time and double-checking the job spec.

It is hard to focus, though. Thoughts racing through my mind. And not the great kind of thoughts. 'I can't do this.' 'I'm not good enough.' 'I'm a failure.' 'I'm worthless.' 'Who do I think I am?' 'Fat, ugly and stupid, yes, that's me.' 'I'm going to fail.'

I'm hearing these thoughts and they are going on and on and on... I ask myself: 'Are these true? Can I not?' I'm so tired and really don't need this right now. Why is it happening now of all times? 'Maybe these are true. Maybe you should forget about it.' Tomorrow is such a big day. Even more thoughts pop in... 'Frederique, I don't know, maybe you can't...'

Can you relate? This is what happens when you go for your goal, the one you've decided to accomplish, and then BANG, this inner dialogue – specifically this negative self-talk, based on your beliefs – kicks in. Most of these stem from your childhood, what you've heard from family members, and you started believing these things. Since then, anytime you are about to do something new, this negative self-talk kicks in to stop you in your tracks. Beliefs are a key part of accomplishing anything in our lives, at work and at home. Your brain needs to believe you *can* before progressing to the next step.

When I talk about inner dialogue, I mean that little voice of yours. *Oh… did you think only you had one?* I have one too. In fact, we all have it. And for years, my voice controlled me. Until I said *'Enough!'* I reached the point where I understood that our inner thoughts control us as long as we let them, and I endeavoured to learn as much as I could to control these. You see, we all have that little voice but we don't all listen to it.

Language is powerful, which is why it's important to pay attention to it. Your brain believes everything you think, explaining why your thoughts either ignite or extinguish your next action. It's therefore vital to learn the strategies to become an expert at controlling your mind, not the other way around. *Be the boss of your mind.*

In order to enable you to do that, I first want to mention something that's a common pitfall: ignoring those thoughts and wishing them away is not an effective strategy. You know, when you say to yourself: '*Ah, I'll just put it to the back of my mind*'? I see you nodding along; of course, I've said that too before. Before I knew how unproductive this was.

Think about this idiom, carefully looking at the language, and ask yourself: '*Where did that negative thought go?*' See, where it went… It did not go away at all: it still is in your mind, specifically the back of your mind, taking up some of your energy. Not only does this not work, but it also has a negative impact all around, as you are not dealing with it at all. Ignoring it does not make it disappear: by doing this, you are letting it hold space and control you.

I hear you say, '*What can I actually do when this happens?*' Let's do it and together discover how to control your inner dialogue so that it stops being destructive and stops preventing you from getting results. These thoughts hold you back from going for what you want. If not addressed, these keep you from accomplishing your goals.

Learning how to believe in yourself and in your ability to accomplish whatever you set your mind to opens you up to the extraordinary. As I often say, *'Absolutely amazing things happen when you believe!'* By forming this series of 3 wires in your brain, you learn how to move from 'Can I?' to 'I CAN!', which is an important success point on your goal-reaching journey.

WIRE 1.1

STRATEGIC CONTROL – STRATEGY: STOP

This is where we are building the first of the 3 *Strategic Control* wires as part of your *Accept with Strategic Control* circuit. As you can see from the highlighted part of this circuit framework in Illustration 4, this is the *Strategic Control – Stop* wire on your path.

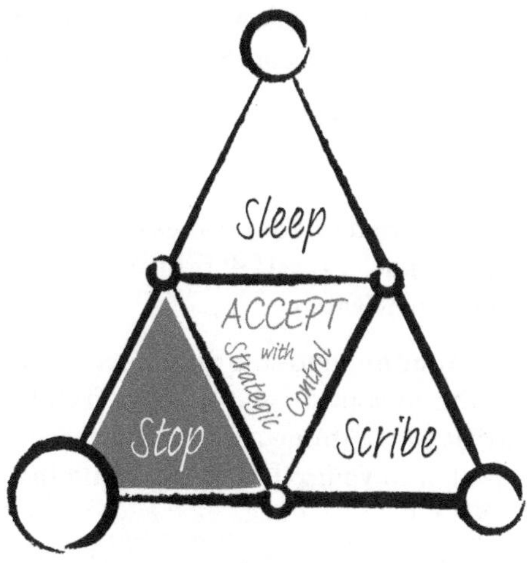

Illustration 4: The *Lead Beyond The Edge* Strategic Control – Stop Wire framework

I have a very personal attachment to this particular strategy – I'm close to all of them and will often mention why when teaching these to you, but this one is that bit extra special. It is the one that I like to think showed me the way forward.

You see, I was in my early twenties and I was rebuilding myself and learning to blossom. Super shy, incredibly introverted, afraid of voicing anything, afraid of my own voice in fact… and yet, I was committed to make it happen. So, on one weekend afternoon, I found myself at a 'Change Your Life' workshop.

At the event, I loved how no one knew me: they didn't know where I came from, they didn't know any of my past, and this really felt freeing. I quietly soaked it all up. It really did start a fire within me. I saw who I always knew I was and yet I had buried her down, way down – that person reminded me of how a very important person in my life saw me.

It clicked. And, wow, those 3 hours showed me the power of our minds and brains, and to this day, 20 years later, I've never stopped continuing my quest to learn as much as I could, so that I could make a difference in the world. And, here we are! I wanted to share this background story with you and now let's talk about this amazingly simple, yet amazingly powerful, strategy to control your inner dialogue.

So, a negative thought comes in and…

STOP!

This is it. A one-word strategy. And it is exactly like it is. Remember how empowering simplicity is. STOP is the strategy to implement as you are building this new wire.

You, commanding your mind to stop with a verbal interruption. You, sending a command to yourself and saying: 'STOP!' This is a direct command, so give it with a strong and firm tone. You can either voice it out loud or speak it to yourself. It has to sound like an order; hear yourself give it: 'STOP!'

You are the boss: direct yourself. You are taking charge by saying 'STOP!'

It worked then and it works now. This was mind-blowing for me. This had been a challenge of mine for years, almost an entire decade of my life, and this one word shifted control over to me. I was in charge of my inner dialogue. As far as I remember, this was the first time in my life. Instead of it running me over, controlling my life, controlling my decisions, controlling my next moves, I was in control. And I've been in charge ever since, using this very practical and effective strategy whenever I need to.

This direct command helps you interrupt this unproductive behaviour. It disrupts it and brings it to a stop, literally and physically.

Science

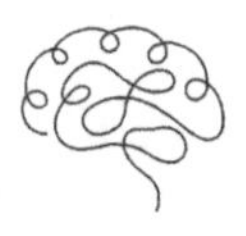

The science behind the effectiveness of this strategy ties back to neuroplasticity and your ability to wire and rewire your brain. When you direct yourself to stop, you interrupt a behaviour – in this specific instance, the behaviour whereby you're holding space for a negative thought.

Unless you do something, that negative thought usually goes to another one and then another one and then another one: it becomes a negative thought loop or a negative thought pattern.

This cognitive strategy, first introduced in the 1950s by Joseph Wolpe, a psychiatrist specializing in behaviour science, is commonly used in behavioural psychology to change a thought pattern behaviour and is referred to as *thought-stopping*, which is in fact a pattern interrupt.

Remember when we spoke about awareness and I shared with you about our 2 minds? This is a great situation to increase your awareness: it requires you to catch yourself in the act, or rather in the thought. Any time you do, you help shift this thought pattern behaviour from unconscious to conscious, and that in itself helps you take charge by interrupting it.

When a group of neurons fire together, they form a thought. The STOP command acts as the trigger to interrupt the self-sabotaging thought. It is like a jolt: it helps you get out of it by interrupting the path in your brain that it usually goes down. See it like this. Usually, up to now really, when you used to have a negative thought come in – let's call that group of neurons, your NT-a (for Negative Thought-a) – it would go from a to b, so go from NT-a to NT-b, adding another negative thought, so firing even more neurons and this is where you would usually spiral down. But now you've learned how neurons communicate and connections form, you understand that path has only become as strong as you let it by repeating it over and over again.

Here I'd like to add something to this strategy and make it even more effective and beneficial to support you along the way. I'm calling it *Stop and Soar*. You see, once you've interrupted the usual path of that negative thought and as you are changing its connections, how about you take it that one step further and create a new connection, so you are not only *rewiring* but also *wiring and forming new connections.*

Let's call it PT-s (for Positive Thought-soar); it started from NT-a, but instead of going to NT-b, thanks to your thought-stopping strategy, you are redirecting it to PT-s, and this is where – you've guessed it from the PT letters – you think of a positive thought. How amazing that you can turn your negative thought loop into a positive one! Replace it with whatever positive thought you want: I suggest you make it short, strong and empowering.

Now, by applying both this pattern interrupt and this pattern replacement, you direct your brain to a different connection point. And, instead of going from NT-a to NT-b, it goes from NT-a to PT-s. As you do this again and again and again, the existing a to b wire will get weaker and weaker every time you apply this strategy, as you are rewiring your brain and leading it to go from NT-a to PT-s, as the new connection gets stronger and stronger. This is Hebb's Rule in action – remember, '*Neurons that fire together wire together*'. So fire it up!

And here you go: you now have this STOP strategy that you can use whenever you need to. You can apply it for any of your goals as this *inner dialogue* challenge comes up for you. Next, the '1.2' wire strategy within this circuit…!

WIRE 1.2

STRATEGIC CONTROL – STRATEGY: SCRIBE

This is where we are building the second of the 3 *Strategic Control* wires as part of your *Accept with Strategic Control* circuit. As you can see from the highlighted part of this circuit framework in Illustration 5, this is the *Strategic Control – Scribe* wire on your path.

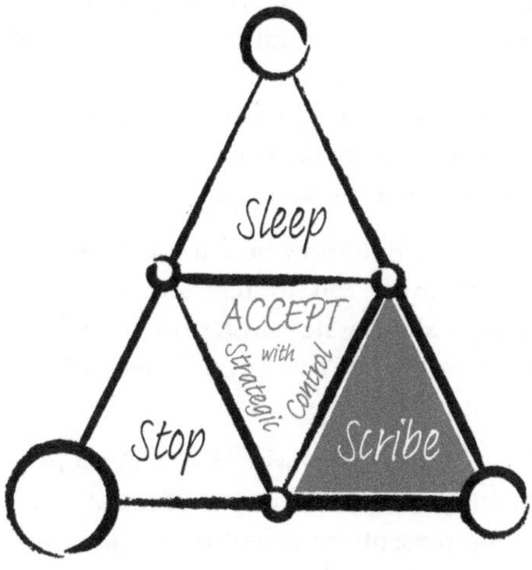

Illustration 5: The *Lead Beyond The Edge* Strategic Control – Scribe Wire framework

In a world where technology abounds, our next wire focuses on an activity that you might not have done in a while. This strategy has successfully been used for centuries and, thanks to neuroimaging techniques, scientific advancements have been made over the last decade, highlighting its effectiveness even more. I'm talking about writing – specifically, writing by hand.

The process of handwriting is so much more powerful than typing for your brain that, to this day, both for and beyond this strategy, I still love to write by hand. Even though I consider myself pretty tech-savvy and I do own a laptop, a phone and a tablet, I write all my ideas and notes on paper first. I also use flipcharts, sticky notes and markers at workshops with my clients. While this may be seen by some as old-fashioned, handwriting is so beneficial for your brain that it has to be one of our strategies.

So, a negative thought comes in and…

SCRIBE!

Now, I hear you ask: '*Frederique, why are you using an old word instead of using the word "write"?*' I'm glad you asked! I'm using the word 'scribe' in place of 'write' as I want to help you remember these strategies within this circuit you are building, and I know that by using a mnemonic device – here, a pattern of the letter S – this will improve your ability to remember this content. Using mnemonic devices, such as alliteration, helps your brain store the information and recall it better as it encodes it in a special way.

While at the time I did not know how it was benefiting my brain and my body, I've been using this strategy for many years. This started because I felt unable and unsafe to voice my thoughts and feelings out loud, so instead I would start writing. I'd journal my thoughts, and this always made me feel better.

Here is how this wire strategy works. Have a pen and paper handy and start writing down your inner dialogue. Write it down exactly as you are thinking it. Be present; be mindful. No filter, no judgement, no censoring. Journal it all.

Not only does your inner dialogue weigh you down, it also makes you stressed, unfocused and unproductive. As long as it stays in your head, it is – as I like to say – a mumbo jumbo mess! Writing it down on paper helps free up space and put thoughts into perspective, thus making these clearer. It is like a decluttering exercise, where you clear it all out, like a brain dump from head to paper.

Your aim here is total honesty and transparency with yourself: what are you thinking, and how are your thoughts making you feel? Write down your thoughts and feelings. This is called *expressive writing*. You express what's on your mind. And this is for your eyes only, so no inhibition – scribe freely.

You know how I like to always give you as much as I can, so I'd like to add a further step here. I call this becoming best friends with your inner saboteur. I use this process with my clients, where I symbolically bring in their best friend; here, let's bring in yours. I want you to use the power of your imagination to see and hear your best friend. What would their reaction be upon reading your inner dialogue? Ask yourself, what would your best friend tell you right now?

Another way to do it is to reverse the roles. Ask yourself: would you talk to your best friend the way that you've just spoken to yourself? No, you would not, and that gives you the perspective you need to stop doing it right now. Truth be told, if anyone was talking to you the way you sometimes talk to yourself, you'd give them a piece of your mind, so stop it (see how we can tie in our first wire strategy here…!).

Of course, by now you already know how beneficial it is to control your inner dialogue. And, as always, within this section I want to bring in the science, so it helps you reinforce all your learnings to date, thus strengthening the wire you've built.

The earliest scientific work on this comes from James Pennebaker, a social psychologist. More recently, over the last decade, Matthew Lieberman, a social psychologist and neuroscientist as well as the founder of social cognitive neuroscience, has continued research that follows in Pennebaker's footsteps. Thanks to Matthew Lieberman and his team of researchers, and the addition of neuroimaging, we continue to learn more about how the brain responds to journaling.

This process is called *affect labelling*. It is such an interesting strategy because you might initially think that spending time on journaling your thoughts and feelings is counterproductive, but that is not true at all. In fact, research has shown the opposite is true. By writing down your thoughts and feelings, you diminish their intensity.

Journaling helps you understand your inner dialogue: it raises your awareness, thus making it more manageable so you can work through it; it also ensures that you are not bottling it up. This strategy helps you gain more control by giving you the skill to self-regulate. It is such a great tool all round, as studies have shown its effectiveness for reducing your stress, boosting your mood, facilitating problem-solving and increasing your performance.

Thanks to neuroimaging, we understand what's going on in our brains during this process. Remember your amygdalae? Here they are at it again! You recall how your amygdalae are involved in your fear and emotional responses, right? And so here, usually your inner dialogue would trigger alarm bells – and you know what happens next with the activation of the threat response and how it makes you feel and impact your next moves. But you now know better thanks to this new wire you've formed, and by executing this strategy, you can control its impact.

When you verbalize your feelings by writing your thoughts down, putting these into words, according to scientists there is a decreased response in the amygdalae. Scans using fMRI – functional magnetic resonance imaging – to study subjects' brain activity showed that the amygdalae were less active. This means that you are less prone to triggering the threat response – and it occurs simply by making the time to write it all down – helping your brain calm down.

Matthew Lieberman (2007) explains the impact of affect labelling by using a traffic light analogy: '*In the same way you hit the brake when you're driving when you see a yellow light, when you put feelings into words, you seem to be hitting the brakes on your emotional responses.*' How amazing that you now know of a way to reduce physiological responses in your body! Can you see how impactful this is for your behaviours?

In addition to noticing a decreased response in the amygdalae, scientists also saw on the scans that the right ventrolateral PreFrontal Cortex (rvlPFC) – located in the frontal lobe of your brain – was activated. It turned down the emotional response to being present in the moment. '*We found the more mindful you are, the more activation you have in the right ventrolateral prefrontal cortex and the less activation you have in the amygdala*' (University of California 2007). This is one of the studies that successfully links mindfulness and neuroscience.

And here you go: you now have this SCRIBE strategy that you can use whenever you need to. You can apply it for any of your goals as this *inner dialogue* challenge comes up for you. Next, the '1.3' wire strategy within this circuit…!

WIRE 1.3

STRATEGIC CONTROL – STRATEGY: SLEEP

This is where we are building the third of the 3 *Strategic Control* wires as part of your *Accept with Strategic Control* circuit. As you can see from the highlighted part of this circuit framework in Illustration 6, this is the *Strategic Control – Sleep* wire on your path.

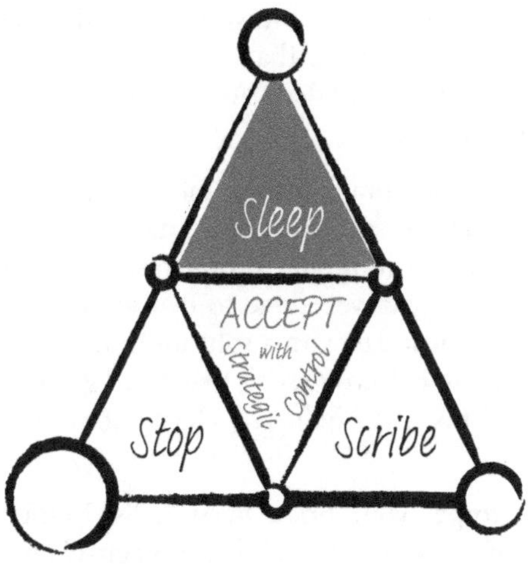

Illustration 6: The *Lead Beyond The Edge* Strategic Control – Sleep Wire framework

This strategy is once again very actionable, but in a sense very different, as for this one you need to let go and trust your brain. Our next wire strategy is to shhhhhh: SLEEP (yes, another S word to complete our inner dialogue wires mnemonic).

Do you ever wonder whether your brain sleeps? It does not: it remains 100% active in order to continue monitoring many of the functions needed for you to operate, including breathing; however, it does need *you* to sleep.

Some people think sleeping robs them of the time to do more, but this could not be further from the truth. Sleep deprivation is not conducive to great results at all. Brain fog makes it hard to think, concentrate, focus, make decisions confidently, lead any type of project assertively or come up with a great creative campaign. It also leaves you moody, anxious, uncoordinated and prone to catching colds and flu as your immune system is weakened. And that's not even all of it.

Simply put, your brain needs its sleep so it can function properly. Sleep helps you to be at your best the next day, ensuring you have optimal access to all the cognitive functions you will need, and this is required day after day. It is a lot more than *just* 'beauty sleep'; instead, start seeing it as your *brain booster* sleep. And, science agrees and continues to prove it again and again.

When you sleep, your brain does a lot! It processes the events of your day, consolidating and connecting memories to help you with memory retention, learning and problem-solving (yes, think about it: how many times have you gone to bed with a problem in mind and woken up the next day with a solution?); it releases proteins and growth hormones to help you repair tissue and grow new cells; it gets rid of waste and toxins to help you clear out your central nervous system.

Plus, let's not forget your brain nerve cells. Remember all those neurons of yours – 86 billion of them? Sleep plays a great role in synaptic plasticity. When you sleep, they restore and repair as well as consolidate and optimize your brain circuitry! It's essential, so that they can continue to communicate and reorganize themselves, supporting you and your goals along the way.

And last but not least, sleep is vital for emotional health, which brings us to controlling our inner dialogue. Here, we are going to talk again about – yes, you've guessed it – your amygdalae! Remember how these are involved in your emotional responses, right? When you are sleep-deprived, your amygdalae are more prone to becoming over-active, while when you sleep well, they get to respond in a more adaptive way, thus allowing you to gain more control.

Out of all the wires that you are learning to build and strengthen on your *Lead Beyond The Edge* bold path, I know this one is already built in! So my focus for you is to ensure that it becomes a habitual wire, one that gets stronger and stronger, so you can benefit cognitively day after day.

One of the very first questions popping into your mind probably has to do with sleep length, right? Ideally, as adults, you want to make time for a 7- to 9-hour sleep night. And here I want to get you to think of your night-time ritual. Do you have one? If not, you should have one. Consistency is important for your goals and indeed your sleep. So whether you already have one, which we can then fine-tune, or you are going to now put one in place, make sure that your existing ritual or the one you are creating from today onwards incorporates the following guidelines:

- Start by picking a regular time for you to sleep – got it? This will ensure that you set your body clock into a rhythm.
- From there, you want to make sure that you eat at least 3 hours before that time, avoiding heavy foods – as digestion will disrupt your sleep – as well as stimulants like caffeine and nicotine; this gives you your dinner limit time.
- It also works the same with physical exercise, so this gives you your exercise limit time.
- Then, you also want to stop any type of blue light, so no TV and put your phone, tablet, laptop and e-reader device away 2 hours before that time; this gives you your gadgets limit time.

Regarding the last guideline, I'd like to add that stopping any type of blue light before bed is the ideal solution, but if you are wondering about a lesser option, you can look at switching on filtering technology often built into the devices or using stick-on filters; both of these will help reduce the blue light emission.

Applying these 4 guidelines will help you wind down to create the best and most restorative sleep environment.

Now that we've covered your sleep ritual, I bet you are wondering, *'But Frederique, what if my inner dialogue makes it hard for me to fall asleep or keeps me tossing and turning?'* I've got you covered! I have a further step for you.

Grab a pen and paper and write down – ideally by hand, as you know it is most effective – 5 things you are grateful for right before switching off your light. I like to start mine with 'I'm grateful for…' and then start each of my 5 bullets points with a verb +ing, so for instance:

I'm grateful for:

- waking up after a great night of sleep
- leading a great consulting session with a client
- having an uninterrupted and fast internet connection during my live keynote
- cycling with the sun shining on my face
- dining out with special friends celebrating a business milestone.

Gratitude is a powerful habit, and one that has been proven to have neural effects in the brain – very much like what we are doing together here, leveraging neuroplasticity and forming circuits and wires to support your goals and lead you to success.

By handwriting your gratitude list before bed, you will experience a faster, better and longer sleep, as well as improve your performance the next day. As for your disruptive inner dialogue, it will be lessened as your brain will be drifting off with thankful thoughts. It is a win-win.

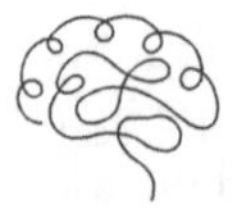

Sleep is a complex science and involves many parts of our brain – the 2 main ones are the hypothalamus, located in your temporal lobe, and the brainstem. I want to stay focused here, and extract and share with you the scientific findings that are going to help you reinforce our wire strategy.

I'll start with sharing a bit more about our sleep cycles. Neuroimaging techniques, particularly fMRI, are used to study brain activity during sleep. Thanks to many studies focusing on brain waves and neuronal activity, scientists have found that there are 5 stages of brain activity during one sleep cycle.

One sleep cycle is about 90 minutes. You go from one cycle to another several times and spend different times at each stage throughout the various cycles during a night's sleep. You can sort out these 5 stages into 2 main categories: Rapid Eye Movement (REM) and Non-Rapid Eye Movement (NREM).

The first 4 stages of one sleep cycle are NREM ones; the first 2 are *light sleep*, while the last 2 are *deep sleep* – these are the most restorative stages. And the fifth stage is your REM one; this is where you dream, learn, consolidate and problem-solve. In keeping with its name, your eyes, behind your closed eyelids, move rapidly from side to side throughout this stage. I also want to add here that your amygdalae – and this will not be surprising, given what we have learned so far about them – are increasingly active during this stage.

Now, how about we discuss the science behind naps too? Yes, you were probably wanting this, right? Naps have been scientifically proven across many studies to increase productivity and mood, thus boosting performance and morale. And, as more scientific advancements continue to be made, it is no surprise that companies such as Apple, Google, Samsung, Ben & Jerry's and NASA have embraced sleep and do let their employees nap at work.

With naps, you want to get their timing as well as their length right to get the most out of them. I'm sure it has happened to you before when you took a nap and, instead of waking up feeling re-energized, you woke up feeling totally out of sorts and to top it all off, you had trouble sleeping that night.

Timing wise, planning your nap too late in the day will interfere with your night schedule, so ideally plan it around midday or after lunch, between 1 pm and 4 pm. Getting the length of your nap wrong will leave you feeling groggy – this is called *sleep inertia*; this grogginess is caused by the fact that you incorrectly timed your nap and woke up during one of the deeper sleep stages, hence the haziness you are experiencing.

I want to cover 2 different nap lengths, so you can pick whichever option will work best for you depending on where you are and what time it is: 15 minutes and 90 minutes. The first one, often referred to as a *power nap*, will go through the first 2 stages of a sleep cycle and increase your energy, alertness, motor skills and cognitive performance. A 90-minute nap will go through a full sleep cycle and it will leave you feeling refreshed and boost memory and creativity, as well as be restorative, helping you recover from a bad night of sleep.

And here you go: you now have this SLEEP strategy that you can use whenever you need to. You can apply it for any of your goals as this *inner dialogue* challenge comes up for you. Next, a surprise section…

You know how practical I want this to be for you, so here, at the end of this circuit – and for the other 2 circuits – you'll find a working example so that you can see how these strategies work practically to tackle an *inner dialogue* challenge thanks to its *Lead Beyond The Edge* solutions.

I'd like to add that there are a multitude of scenarios on your goal journey. Thanks to the stories and anecdotes in this book, you're already discovering how the framework works for absolutely any of your goals: anything, anytime, anywhere in both your professional and personal life. So next, for these bonus sections, I've picked 3 business-related scenarios for you to experience how to apply these wire strategies and their effects once activated.

1

Let's fire it up!

Wire 1.1: Strategic Control – Strategy: Stop

Wire 1.2: Strategic Control – Strategy: Scribe

Wire 1.3: Strategic Control – Strategy: Sleep

Scenario ▶ Launch a new project in front of your leadership team.

You've worked hard on this new project and it is time to officially launch it. Your manager has asked you to lead the launch and present it to the leadership team. You want to do it BUT you find yourself crippled with destructive inner dialogue: *'I'm going to be a disaster.' 'What if I forget what to say?' 'I cannot stand up in front of all of those people, they are going to think I'm stupid.' 'I'm not good enough.' 'I'm going to fail.'*

The 1.1 solution
▶ *Activate the STOP wire strategy.*

Find a quiet spot and say 'STOP!' Remember, this direct command will interrupt this destructive inner dialogue. Plus, you can Stop and Soar, and also say: *'I can do this!'* Yes, you can: remind yourself that you've created this project from nothing; you know all of its ins and outs, and it is ready to be launched to support your team members.

The 1.2 solution
▶ *Activate the SCRIBE wire strategy.*

Grab a pen and paper or your journal and SCRIBE. Write down your inner dialogue by hand. Write it down as it comes up for you in total honesty and transparency. Ask yourself: *'What am I thinking?'* and *'How is it making me feel?'* and write it all down. Once this is done, you can also think of your best friend, and ask yourself, *'What would they tell me right now if they could read what I'm thinking of myself?'*

The 1.3 solution
▶ *Activate the SLEEP wire strategy.*

Go to bed at your usual time to ensure a 7- to 9-hour sleep night; you've also eaten and last exercised 3 hours ago and have stopped any type of blue light 2 hours ago. As you are winding down, you grab a pen and paper and write down 5 things for which you are grateful. Since the upcoming launch presentation is on your mind, you decide to focus on 5 things you are grateful for at work. Then SLEEP. Let go and trust your brain to help you process all the information and as you wake up the next day, you will be at your best with optimal access to all of the cognitive functions you need.

Any and all of these strategies are helping you gain strategic control as you take charge and push through your comfort zone. You are doing it: you are leading beyond the edge, and launching this new project in front of your leadership team.

YOU CAN!

And *voilà*, there you have them: my 3 actionable strategies to help you control your inner dialogue. If your thoughts get in the way, **STOP, SCRIBE** and **SLEEP** your way to strategic control to reach your 'I CAN!' success point. Each of these represents one of the *Strategic Control* wires as part of our first circuit, which you've now entirely built!!!

You will find a recap text version of what you've accomplished in the next section. As for now, I know you are expecting me to close a certain story I opened at the beginning of this *Strategic Control* circuit, right? So, where were we? *Here I was, on a high stool at the kitchen counter, being controlled by my inner dialogue…*

Story

'Preparing for a job interview and grounding myself!'

As soon as I heard myself say these words, I caught myself in the act and this is exactly what I needed. I distinctly and firmly uttered the word 'STOP!' I closed the computer, gathered all my notes and put them in the folder I'd be carrying with me at the interview tomorrow.

I deserved that job interview and I knew it was within my control to be at my best and demonstrate how I was the best person for the role. I collected my thoughts and got ready for bed: winding down, powering all gadgets off and grabbing my book. After one hour or so of reading, I put the book down and grabbed my journal to write 5 things I was most grateful for today. Counting blessings and sheep, I fell asleep.

Waking up the next day after a great night of sleep, I got ready and headed to the company headquarters. To this day, I can still remember muttering under my breath, 'Frederique, you can do this!' as I passed the threshold of the large and light boardroom, where I had 3 back-to-back interviews. And even more detailed and fresh in my mind is the phone call the following week, letting me know I had the job and that they looked forward to welcoming me as their European Communication Leader.

RECAP CIRCUIT 1/3

ACCEPT with STRATEGIC CONTROL

WooHoo!
(I say that on stage, so it feels natural to write it for you too.)

You have built your first circuit and its 4 wires!!! This is definitely a cause for celebration as it gets you closer to extraordinary results (and a small teaser: you will soon discover that celebrating your achievements along the way has been scientifically proven to be an effective strategy, so go on – do it!).

You have used the power of your mind to rewire your brain to create your very first circuit and its 4 wires as part of your *Lead Beyond The Edge* bold path. Now continue to strengthen it with repetition every time you activate it. With neuroplasticity, the more times you do it, the fewer times you'll have to do it!

Here is a recap text version of what you've accomplished.

Let's Fire It ALL Up!

Lead Beyond The Edge, Circuit 1/3

Activate your first circuit
to help you strengthen your beliefs,
control your inner dialogue and move from…

Can I?

ACCEPT with Strategic Control

- Overarching Wire 1: Accept
    - Intro Wires: Strategic Control
        - Wire 1.1: Strategic Control – Strategy: Stop
        - Wire 1.2: Strategic Control – Strategy: Scribe
        - Wire 1.3: Strategic Control – Strategy: Sleep
- Recap Circuit 1/3: Accept with Strategic Control

… to

I CAN!

Multisensory Learning Boosts: Circuit 1/3

Remember how I surprised you in the *Launch Circuit* by announcing that you would be doing more with this book than *just* reading? Here is where it practically unfolds. This is the first series of *multisensory learning boosts* for you to implement, and as a result deepen your learning, thus strengthening these newly built pathways in your brain even more.

First, we are going to engage and boost your olfactory sense.

Your olfactory sense is particularly powerful; in fact, you already know that, although you might not be consciously aware of it yet…! Let me guide you: have you ever smelled something and instantly been transported to a very vivid memory of yours? You have, right? It is because odours can trigger memories. For me, the smell of lavender instantly transports me to my childhood at my grandparents' house, specifically playing besides Grand-Mère's resting chair, feeling her calm warm gaze on me.

This is called the *Proust Effect*, named after the novelist Marcel Proust, who in 1913 described this phenomenon in the opening chapter of one of his books by sharing how a tea-soaked madeleine cake brought him back to his childhood, explaining how he was able to suddenly remember his aunt's house in remarkable detail.

We have known about this for centuries, but weren't sure why it happens. Thanks to neuroimaging techniques, we now know. Our olfactory system, located in the temporal lobe, processes information received from neurons – olfactory receptor ones – in the nose, which travel first to our emotion centre (your amygdalae) and then to our memory centre (your hippocampus). It is the only sense that directly connects to these centres.

So let's leverage all of this and use this powerful sense to help you strengthen your learning by facilitating increased retention and productivity.

Ready? Let's boost your learning using your olfactory sense:

As the first step is picking a scent, the question on your lips… is, *'Frederique, which scent do I pick?'* You can train your brain to respond to any scent, so I encourage you to pick one you like and *that one* will work for you. If you aren't sure, research has revealed that lavender, rosemary and peppermint can help you learn better by enhancing focus, concentration and memory.

- Pick a scent of your choice, something you can easily access – in my trainings, I bring with me a set of 12 essential oils so that my trainees can pick the aroma of their choice and it is easy for them to buy it once they are back at work to continue cueing: lavender, vanilla, cedarwood, lemon, peppermint, rosemary…
- Smell it (inhale or diffuse) and reflect on this particular circuit and its wires, and their teachings (which have now been stored as memories in your brain) and write down 3 to 5 insights you've gained as you've built your first circuit: think of the 4 strategies: Accept + Stop, Scribe, Sleep; alternate scent and writing – this will help you to associate the scent you've chosen with your learning.
- Then, sleep: remember how efficient your brain is when you sleep? We spoke about it as part of one of the wires you built on your path. This is when memory consolidation happens, and that's why we are adding sleep to our sensory learning boost as it has been scientifically proven that odour cues help to optimize learning during sleep.
- Enjoy and repeat!

Using a scent as a stimulus, you've learned how to trigger a *Lead Beyond The Edge* memory, a particular series of insights you had gained as you read and built your first circuit and its wires. Trigger it again and again by simply smelling your scent, thus reinforcing the pathways in your brain.

Second, we are going to engage and boost your tactile sense.

Did you know that the sense of touch is the first one we develop? As a tactile person, I've always had a special connection with my sense of touch, so it was music to my ears – and indeed tingles in my fingers – to discover that our learning can be reinforced by movement.

This technique is called *anchoring*, and even though you can set anchors in all sensory systems, here we will focus and develop a series of kinaesthetic anchors to help you anchor your insights and help you fire your *Lead Beyond The Edge* path whenever you want to.

The kinaesthetic anchor can be a movement or a touch. Research has shown that learning is enhanced when it involves both mind and body. I really like this quote from neurophysiologist and educator Carla Hannaford: *'Movement anchors thought.'* This can be explained by looking at the anatomy of your brain, as the cerebellum is the brain area involved in both learning and motor control.

You might have heard of anchoring before as one of the techniques taught in self-help trainings using Neuro-Linguistic Programming, or NLP, a series of techniques for self-improvement created by John Grinder and Richard Bandler in the 1970s. Anchoring is one of these techniques that is rooted in science.

Indeed, scientifically, you may already know where anchoring comes from if you've heard of the scientific experiment of psychologist Ivan Pavlov in the late 1800s; his studies involved a bell, dogs and food. He was able to train the dogs so that when they heard the bell, they'd associate it with eating and start salivating. He managed to condition their brains to think that upon the bell ringing, food would be served. Anchoring can also be called *conditioning* or *stimulus-response*.

Anchoring is the conditioning of the nervous system and a form of associative learning; it is connecting one thing to another since memory is associative. To anchor, you need 2 components: a state and a stimulus. With anchoring, you teach your brain to recall a state, which you trigger thanks to a stimulus. These 2 components become associated and linked neurologically. Remember, Hebb's Rule!

Here your state is 'Accept with Strategic Control' and your stimulus is your kinaesthetic anchor. Having fully embraced this strategy, over the years I've set a handful of kinaesthetic anchors that I fire whenever I need them; next time you see me live, see whether you can spot what I do every single time as I step on stage! So, let's leverage this knowledge to help you strengthen your learning by facilitating increased retention and wellbeing.

Ready? Let's boost your learning using your tactile sense:

- Elicit the desired state. I'm going to give you 2 steps – the stronger your state, the stronger the anchor.
- *First step:* Read out loud the 3 to 5 insights you've compiled as part of our first learning boost; make sure these start with 'I…' to fully engage with them; this is about eliciting your state, so go beyond reading and perform these to really feel the impact of your insights.
- As you do that, it is time to set your first kinaesthetic anchor, the one I've created for you for this first circuit and its wires. To form it, firmly press the tip of your thumb to the tip of your forefinger (pick whichever hand you prefer); press and pulse it a dozen times while reading your notes.
- *Second step:* Recall a time when you believed you could, when it felt like: 'Yes, I CAN!' and then you moved forward to achieve your goal. Got it? Step into the memory and be as descriptive as possible. What does it feel like? What do you see? Hear? Touch? Maybe even smell and taste? Feel it throughout your body.
- As you do that, repeat your anchor: press firmly the tip of your thumb to the tip of your forefinger; press and pulse it a dozen times while reliving your memory.
- Release your anchor when you feel at your best, when the peak of the intensity is reached.
- (Optional) When I first form my own anchors, I like to also add some music to intensify the experience even more, so how about playing in the background one of your favourite energizing songs as you create your anchor?
- Test it. To do so, you first have to break your state, which I can help you do by asking you a question that's going to get you to think of something else: so tell me, what was the colour of your first car? Now that the state has been broken, it is time to fire your anchor. Two things can happen: you will either recall that state or just not yet; most anchors need a couple of times to be fully formed, so simply repeat the process.
- Enjoy and repeat!

Using a movement as a stimulus, you've learned how to trigger one of your *Lead Beyond The Edge* states, a particular series of insights you had gained as you read and built your first circuit and its wires. Trigger it again and again by simply firing your anchor, thus reinforcing the pathways in your brain.

And third, last but not least, we are going to engage and boost your auditory sense.

As children, our imagination was a normal part of our daily routines; as adults, some have stopped using that powerful tool. Others – Olympians come to mind – leverage the power of their imagination by using it as part of their goal-reaching journey. You can often hear them share how they visualize their race, simulating competition, during their post-win interviews.

Visualizations are a form of meditation, where you actively imagine. As it combines the practice of meditation with the technique of visualization, it is referred to as *visualization meditation*. The operative word here is *actively*: yes, it is an active form, so if you were thinking that I was about to ask you to sit still and focus on your breathing, not quite – there is more. Now, I personally do that too as I meditate daily, as it supports me and my brain, but here I want to especially focus on the power of visualization, as I guide you to make the most of it thanks to your auditory sense.

I have to tell you: I LOVE visualizations! To this day, I still remember my first one. I had never experienced anything like it before and decided then to learn as much as possible about them, so that I'd gain the skills to be able to offer similar experiences to my own clients.

Ever since, I have been doing that; I love incorporating visualization experiences into my work, leveraging its power to help my clients more easily access their own resources and boost their states. I believe in them so much that I listen to my own visualizations. My 'Reach New Heights' audio track, produced to feel clearer, more focused, full of energy and confidence, is a key mindful habit in my success routine.

I hear you ask, '*What happens in my brain when I visualize?*' Scientific findings are astonishing: when you imagine achieving a goal and let yourself feel what it will feel like when you do it, your brain creates that mental imagery and stores it as a memory. *Wait, what?* Yes, you read that correctly: no wonder I've been using the word 'powerful'! (As a little teaser, I want to say here that I share with you even more of the science behind visualization in our second circuit.)

When you visualize something, you stimulate the same brain regions as if you were actually *doing* that something. I used this scientific insight as I lay in bed, having fully dislocated my kneecap: I imagined bending my knee for 10 minutes per day throughout my recovery time, which according to my medical team was significantly accelerated.

Repeatedly imagining having achieved your desired goals in your mind first is an impactful strategy, as your brain then believes that you have done it before and eases you in when you encounter the real thing, making it easier for you. That memory becomes a beacon, helping you feel clearer and more focused about your goal, thus making it more real, approachable and attainable to you.

Thanks to fMRI scans, scientists have found that visualization meditation can alter the brain. Yes, you can drive neuroplasticity here too! The neurological benefits that we have so far found go from increasing connectivity between brain regions to reducing activity in the medial PreFrontal Cortex (mPFC). This brain region has been referred to as the 'Me Centre', as it helps you to process information directly relating to you, from your perspective, to your experiences.

Your mPFC is located in your frontal lobe and is responsible for complex thinking and changing your brain's volume of grey matter. Specifically, there is a noticeable increase in cortical thickness in the hippocampus (remember here, it is an active player in learning and memory) and a decrease in neural activity in the amygdalae (and here they are at play again, helping you process fear and emotional responses).

When engaging in this mindfulness technique, the neural connections in the 'Me Centre' become weaker while the neural connections in your lateral PreFrontal Cortex (lPFC) become stronger. This brain region has been referred to as the 'Assessment Centre', as it is responsible for your reasoning.

These changes allow you to gain better control of your reactions. Basically, you are less 'in your head', reacting less personally and more rationally. Absolutely phenomenal, right? So, let's leverage this knowledge to help you strengthen your learning by facilitating focus, drive and wellbeing.

Ready? Let's boost your learning using your auditory sense! I've especially created an accompanying audio visualization for you to listen to; you will find information about how to access online this additional sensory learning boost within the *Resources* section at the end of the book.

Once you have downloaded it, do the following:

- Set aside 15 minutes.
- Seat yourself in a comfortable and undisturbed place.
- Have your computer or your phone with you on do-not-disturb, so you can access the visualization, but make sure you have turned off emails and any social media alerts so that you maximize your experience.
- Listen to it. You don't need to do anything else, as I will guide you to reflect on this first circuit and its wires helping you think back over your learning and reinforce insights you've gained.
- (Optional) If you are like me and some of my clients, you will want to write down some of the thoughts that popped up during this experience, so you will need this next step. Capture what came up – thoughts, decisions, actions – to continue leading you on your goal journey.
- Enjoy and repeat!

This was yet another way to help you boost your learning as you build your *Lead Beyond The Edge* path; here you have learned how to use your auditory power to reinforce the particular series of insights you gained as you read and built your first circuit and its wires. Trigger it again and again by simply listening to this visualization, thus reinforcing the pathways in your brain.

And this wraps up your first circuit, with its **ACCEPT** overarching wire and its 3 *Strategic Control* wires, **STOP, SCRIBE** and **SLEEP**, as part of your *Lead Beyond The Edge* bold path. Next, you are going to discover how to build your second circuit to continue to lead you to extraordinary results.

As for now, I know you are expecting me to close a certain story I opened at the beginning of this ACCEPT circuit, right? So, where were we? *Here I was, on the edge of the Mendenhall Glacier, wondering whether I should stay back or push through…*

Story
'Hiking to an Alaskan glacier and exploring inside!'

I was scared. At that moment, I knew it was all up to me: I could let my fear win by taking over and stay behind on the edge of the glacier or I could lead beyond the edge and join our expert guide for our ice exploration.

Looking at the magnificent glacier in front of me, I distinctively remember making the time to consciously pause. This was one of those moments where it was important to make the time to recognize that all of those body reactions were normal, as I had never in my life been on a glacier about to explore its features, so I believed it was normal, I gave myself a break and I accepted.

As soon as I did that, having accepted what was going on for what it was and not letting my fear control my next move, my breathing steadied, my muscles relaxed and my heart rate stabilized. And that made my surroundings sparkle even more: all of those ice crystals were stunningly blue. What a truly amazing place to be; I had reached it, and wow, the beauty all around me was everything that I could have ever imagined and more. This definitely was one of those pinch-me moments.

By then, my inner dialogue had shifted to, 'Oh yes, Frederique, you absolutely can do this!' And, with a smile on my face, I let Naomi tighten my microspikes straps. This was thrilling. Seconds away from our exploration. I was doing it. Stomping away on the Mendenhall Glacier. Everywhere I looked was simply spectacular.

And then, to top it all off, with a mysterious smile on her face, our guide told us she had a surprise – due to the constantly changing nature of the glacier and the hazards of the day itself, I knew the tour could not guarantee any specific features, such as ice caves and moulins, as every day is different and such and such feature may not be accessible, so believe me, I was all ears…

My heart skipped a beat as she announced that a few hours before our arrival, a scout guide had determined that in today's conditions, it was safe for us to explore an ice conduit. Ouh là là! *It was so large, that not only did I get to see it, but I went inside it and stood in it in complete awe taking it all in. I will never ever forget that goal moment.*

ADOPT with INSPIRING RESILIENCE CIRCUIT 2/3

Adopting your fear means fighting and pushing through your comfort zone, going for that goal of yours.

You are on a roll!

This is where you continue making it all happen.

You have identified your goal, are ready to accomplish it and you believe you can.

You are at the 'I CAN!' stage.

When I think about this stage, I feel on top of the world, like I can accomplish anything, and the world is my oyster. I believe it with every fibre in my being and this spurs me on. This self-belief acts as a catalyst to making all of my dreams happen. Since my reality is shaped by what I believe in, this point always feels crystal clear. My mind and brain both feel sharper, as if all of the fog has lifted.

I know you've been there before too, thinking of how much closer that goal of yours is by now. Now it is your turn to access that feeling too, very similarly to how we did it for our first circuit. So again here, close your eyes if you wish and imagine how it is going to feel when you accomplish your goal. This time, surprise yourself by how much sharper your visualization is. As you go through the same questions, focus on all of the extra details you are now visualizing: What does it feel like? What do you see? Hear? Touch? Maybe even smell and taste? Got it? Open your eyes. What a feeling, right?

And then, BANG, something happens: it can be so many things, from a pandemic to an earthquake, or from dislocating your kneecap to being bullied by your boss. And, if we've already had the pleasure to meet at an event, you know that none of these examples was picked randomly: these have happened to me and I share these stories from stage. You know what I'm getting at, right? Things happen in our lives, which are so disruptive to our plans that suddenly you find yourself asking, 'Do I have what it takes?'

This is where the second circuit comes in as part of your *Lead Beyond The Edge* path: the one where you and I are going to build the series of wires in your brain to create the new neural pathways that are necessary to take you from this 'Do I have it?' stage to our second success point on your journey as you reach your 'I CAN-DO it!' stage.

'Attitude is a paintbrush.
It colors everything!'
Antoine de Saint-Exupéry

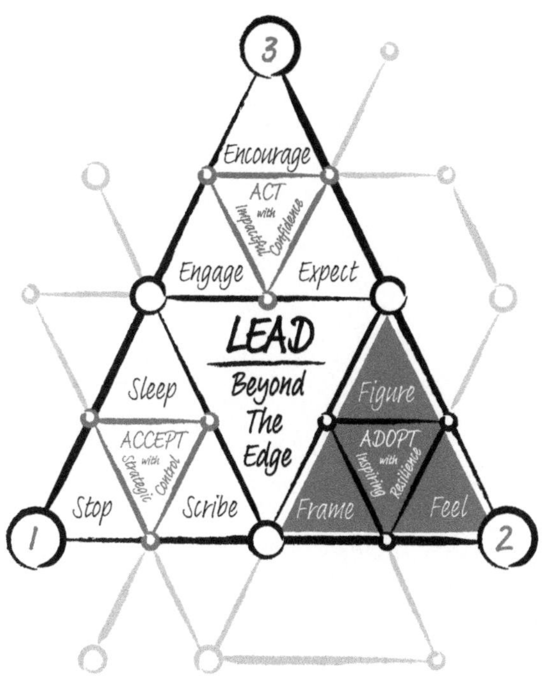

Illustration 7: The *Lead Beyond The Edge* Adopt with Inspiring Resilience Circuit framework

This second circuit has everything to do with your attitudes. You will learn how to convince your brain that you do have it, as well as understand why you have to do this in the first place, expanding your brain knowledge. You will also know what to do in order to strengthen your resilience so that you keep going no matter what happens.

Remember, the success key leading you to extraordinary results, in an approach that is both results-driven and mindful, is focusing on that 'I'm doing it' flow. Upon building that second circuit and implementing these 3 actionable strategies, there will be no stopping you in your tracks at this stage.

Ready? Let's build it!

From 'Do I have it?' to 'I CAN-DO it!'

OVERARCHING WIRE 2

ADOPT

Story 

'Stepping up to help a friend...'

As I was wrapping up my week, on a chilly yet sunny Friday afternoon, my phone beeped as a text message came in. It was from one of my closest friends – she is also one of my peers on the speaking circuit. It said, 'Frederique, I'm sick. Might you be able to go to Seville, Spain from Sunday to Tuesday, to deliver my sessions for MPI?'

Although my first thought was for my friend, I quickly realized what was going on. Being so sick that you cannot show up for one of your booked events is one of our nightmares as professional speakers, as well as for the event meeting planner. I knew this was one of those moments to step up – not only to help a friend, but also support a client. Years of experience on the circuit had led me to believe that I could make it happen. So, after a few short hours, I responded: 'Yes, I can-do it.'

In the meantime, my friend had reached out to the client, explaining her unfortunate situation, and proposed that I replace her for her session at the event. She explained that we had been working together for many years and that she fully trusted me to deliver in her place. Lori, the Head of Meeting Innovation for MPI, was relieved and grateful; she responded positively and the solution fell into place.

After a whirlwind of 39 hours – from sorting out the logistics to prepping everything that usually takes me weeks of preparation for an event, as well as meeting Lori for the very first time via a video call – I found myself on my way to the airport on a Sunday morning. Overnight, a storm had formed, Storm Ciara, which turned out to be an extratropical cyclone, and the atmosphere was very eerie. I remember thinking, 'Everything is going to be okay.'

But this turned out to be the most horrendous travel experience of my life. And I travel a lot. Flights were delayed. The storm got bigger. Flights were cancelled. My bag got lost. There were countless queues. The itinerary changed. The bag was recovered. And after what felt like walking an entire marathon at Dublin Airport (and I did run an actual one!), I found myself at the ticket desk, where the only option available to me was to go to Madrid and from there find my own way to Seville. This meant boarding a flight not knowing how to reach the client's venue, hoping the weather would not get any worse.

It was in that queue that I felt vulnerable. I was tired. It had been non-stop since that text message came in, eyes on the prize. And, what a goal it was! Most speakers work hard to secure an MPI event – Meeting Professionals International is the largest meeting and event industry association globally, and its events are illustrious. I wanted to make it work, and had done so, decision after decision, action after action since Friday afternoon, but at that moment I caught myself thinking, 'I don't know if I have it in me...'

Strategy

As we continue on this journey of achievement, our second circuit is going to be focusing on our attitudes. Remember how I said that 'everything we want to achieve starts in our brain, ignited and fuelled by our beliefs'? Yes? And now, we can add 'supported and influenced by our attitudes'.

So, as we continue this journey, your second mission is going to be to prepare yourself so that you can continue no matter what happens. It is about adopting that can-do attitude that supports you to always keep going and bounce back to make it happen. This is where you can take charge and build your ADOPT circuit, so you can continue directing your brain to go up the path YOU lead it to!

This is where we are building the second of the 3 *Lead Beyond The Edge* circuits. As you can see from the highlighted part of this circuit framework in Illustration 8, this is the *Adopt with Inspiring Resilience* circuit, and for now we are going to focus on the *Adopt* part of it and build that overarching wire on your path.

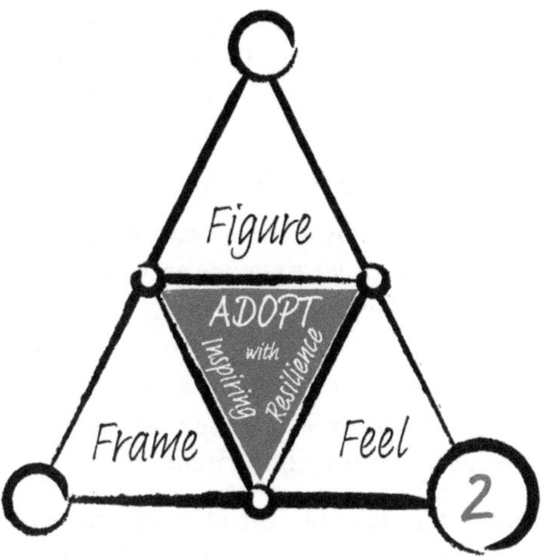

Illustration 8: The *Lead Beyond The Edge* Adopt Wire framework

Now that you have accepted your fear, accepted where you are at and accepted what is going on in your brain and body and why, the next step for you to move forward is to adopt your fear. I can see the corner of your mouth rising and probably thinking: *'Mmmm… Frederique, I've accepted all of that, but I'm not sure how to move towards embracing it… That feels too much of a stretch… How am I supposed to adopt that?'*

Making the decision to adopt this stage of the journey leads you to embrace this new portion of your journey, thus bringing you closer to your goal. I'm going to teach you the way to achieve this and this is going to hit all of the great and exciting notes, while being backed up by science, so you will understand the impact and benefits of this strategy on your brain.

The key is about finding out the way to encourage your brain to hop onboard your vision, and once onboard, support you to that next step.

Adopting is the second overarching wire on our bold path.

And it is all about attitudes. I cannot write any more about this topic without sharing something with you about one of the most influential people in my life regarding attitudes. This person was my grand-father – I called him Grand-Père – and as a child and teenager, he was one of the most important people in my life; he still is, in my heart forever. And I have to tell you – what an attitude towards life he had!

Grand-Père was what you would call today a serial entrepreneur, and he kept going through all the ups and downs in his business adventures. Remember when I said that many of our beliefs are rooted in our childhood? There is no doubt that his presence and love (sometimes tough love!) in my life hugely impacted my beliefs and attitudes.

It is important to raise our awareness towards the major influences in our life growing up in order to assess and identify the beliefs and attitudes we want to continue holding onto. Your beliefs lead to the development and adoption of your attitudes. And, very similarly to our beliefs, we choose our attitudes, and can collapse, form and reinforce attitudes at any time – as we are doing right now, building our Adopt wire as part of our second circuit.

My conscious understanding of attitudes was particularly increased during my social psychology studies over 2 decades ago. When my teacher taught me about attitudes, it simply made so much sense to me, and believe me I wish from the bottom of my heart that I could have reached out to Grand-Père and said: '*Merci!!!*'

My teacher used Gordon Allport's (1935, p. 810) definition of attitude, which I'd like to also share with you now: '*A mental and neural state of readiness, organized through experience, exerting a directive or dynamic influence upon the individual's response to all objects and situations with which it is related.*'

See what I mean? That is how crucial your attitudes are on your journey. Your attitudes define your success. I've always been fascinated by our language and the words we use, and often check out the etymology of a word. Did you know that the word 'attitude' comes from the 1660s, meaning 'posture or position of a figure in a statue or painting' via French *attitude*, from Italian *attitudine*, 'disposition, posture'; also 'aptness, promptitude' from the Late Latin *aptitudinem*? Your attitudes determine how you both approach situations and how you interpret these situations.

I understand that it may feel jarring to move from acceptance to adoption, yet I know I can clarify this for you, so you are able to do it. By now, you already know how much I believe in our power and responsibility in life and in leveraging this ability of ours to make it happen by taking charge. Your attitude is entirely your choice. You have the power to adopt the can-do attitude that will move you towards the results you want.

The reason why it feels odd right now is that you carry with you your previous experiences surrounding fear and the idea to adopt it sounds a bit too much of a stretch as it stands like that. I'd like you to start looking at fear differently.

What if you could look at fear as excitedly as a child is looking through a candy shop window? That would be amazing, right? Can you imagine that child, or even yourself, looking through a candy shop window? Their nose pressed up against the window, sparkling eyes, wide smile, open hands, bursting with excitement!

I believe that fear is just as exciting!!! And that belief sure serves me well again and again and again. You see, it is exciting because fear is a sign that you are about to reach a new level in life. That in itself is cause for celebration, so excitement is a must. By deciding to reach a new altitude at work and at home, you instigated that perceived threat – which you now recognize, acknowledge and accept for what it is – and adopting your fear is the appropriate next step.

Adopting means that you are embracing how your fear symbolizes an imminent jump to a better you. Can you see how this is a different way to look at it? Cognitively, we can always attribute whichever meaning we decide to anything. So, it is up to you, right here, right now, to decide that the fear you are experiencing means that indeed you are on your way to a new level, and that IS exciting.

Fear is only your enemy as long as you dread it, so befriend it today to support you on your success. And that is adoption.

Think about it this way too, and this comes from me consulting and teaching neuromarketing to client groups. If fear was a product, here is how the marketing department would sell it to you so that your brain adopts it. They know that for you to adopt the new product will require you to make a change that they know will create discomfort. So they start by increasing your awareness and list all the problems of the current product, which instinctively helps to move you towards being attracted to the new product, as it provides you with all the solutions to these problems, which proves its value to you. From awareness to interest, evaluation and conversion.

The value of the new product must outweigh the value of the old product. In the very same way, the value of the new attitude must outweigh the value of the old attitude. Not adopting your fear means you are freezing and falling back into your comfort zone, giving up on that goal of yours. Adopting your fear means fighting and pushing through your comfort zone, going for that goal of yours.

With your can-do attitude, you set the tone for your success as it affects everything that you are, have and do. By making the decision to adopt a can-do attitude, you open yourself up to tremendous growth as this attitude takes you even closer to the edge of your comfort zone. And, that's okay, right? It *is* time to stop playing small and safe, and start playing big and bold!

This new attitude of yours of adopting the change gives you the upper hand over your brain as you help it embrace the fear. Talking about helping you, let's add the science behind it, so I can continue increasing your awareness and at the same time reinforce this new attitude of yours. Once the science is fully laid out, you'll be completely convinced that proceeding with adoption is the right next step.

Science

I'm passionate about our brains – no surprise there – and I did write that I'd tell you about a few brain-blowing facts while we build the *Lead Beyond The Edge* framework together. Here I'm going to share with you one of my absolute favourite ones. I particularly love it as it is very quirky, and I love that I can share this with you so in turn you can make this brain quirk work for you.

This is further proof of how powerful your mind is, and right now we want to strengthen the ADOPT wire you are building as part of your second circuit. I cannot think of anything better than leveraging this scientific insight to help you do exactly that.

The earliest mention we can find of this quirk is from Maxwell Maltz, who wrote about it in his *Psycho-Cybernetics* book in 1960. And this ground-breaking insight was scientifically proven decades later by neuroscientists with the help of neuroimaging techniques to document their findings, specifically the plastic changes in the brain.

While you may not have heard of Maxwell Maltz or his book before, chances are high that you've already benefited from his ideas, as these are still considered by many to be foundational within the personal development field.

Which is why I used the word 'ground-breaking'. So, without further ado, here is this fantastic quirk. Did you know that your brain does not know the difference between real and imaginary? It is true. According to Maltz (1960): *'Your nervous system cannot tell the difference between an imagined experience and a "real" experience. In either case, it reacts automatically to information which you give to it from your forebrain. Your nervous system reacts appropriately to what "you" think or imagine to be true. You act, and feel, not according to what things are really like, but according to the image of what your mind holds they are like.'*

Let this sink in... your brain cannot tell the difference between what is real and what is imaginary. What a quirk, isn't it? One of my favourite studies proving this point scientifically has to do with playing on the piano. As a player and a teacher myself – yes, off stage I love teaching children music and piano – this study is particularly close to my heart and I often pick it and share it from stage. I remember teaching, in partnership with *Synaptic Potential*, a module on positive neuroscience to a group of attendees at Bangor University in the United Kingdom, and the looks on the leaders' faces were priceless when I shared the findings.

In this study, a team of neuroscientists asked groups to learn a 5-finger piano exercise: one group learned it physically – that is, they played it over and over again on a piano – while the other group learned it mentally – that is, they played it in their mind over and over again. When transcranial magnetic stimulation (TMS) was used to study the role of plastic changes, the results were astonishing – although not surprising, since Maxwell Maltz had written about it 35 years before. In the words of Alvaro Pascual-Leone (1995), one of the scientists involved in this study at Harvard Medical School, '*mental practice alone led to the same plastic changes in the motor system as those occurring with the acquisition of the skill by repeated physical practice*'.

How fascinating is that?!?! '*Mental practice resulted in a similar reorganization of the brain*' (Pascual-Leone 1995). Wow, wow, WOW! Bringing this back to you and your amazing brain: you can-do it too. And that is the easiest and super fun way to make your brain adopt this next move of your journey.

Let's do it! You are in very good company, as this technique has been used by athletes for several decades with extraordinary results – champions, in both physical and mental sports, from boxing to chess, such as Muhammad Ali, Kayla Harrison, Jack Nicklaus, Missy Franklin Johnson, Tiger Woods, Michael Phelps, Michael Jordan, Natan

Sharansky, all credit their success to *mental rehearsal*. By imagining that you have already done your 'it' goal, your brain will believe that you've done it before and will ease you in when you do it for real.

Remember your missing bookmark? Linking this with our previous circuit, you are now at the stage of your journey where you are about to create that bookmark for your brain, which means you are creating the path that your amygdalae will thereafter be happy to follow when they need it too: this is powerful, isn't it? Neuroplasticity at its best. Albert Einstein said: *'Your imagination is your preview of life's coming attractions.'* Isn't that the truth: scientifically and excitedly!!!

Okay, so, have your goal in mind... got it? This is a 2-step process. First, connect with that goal of yours, specifically with people who have already reached it. You can connect directly or indirectly. Sometimes, for some of our goals, we will know exactly who to speak to and be able to do so; at other times, we have to be more resourceful and maybe read their goal story in a book or a magazine, or watch videos and interviews about them having reached their goal. The outcome of this first step is for you to gather as many details as you can about what it means to reach that goal. Once you've done your research, you are ready for Step 2.

Second, you are going to build your own mental picture. So, eyes closed or eyes open – it's up to you, whichever makes you most comfortable – think of your goal as if you've already accomplished it. This is it: you did it. Imagine you are now the one who has achieved it. Thanks to your preparation, you are able to imagine this vividly and in great detail, so include as many senses as you can. What will you experience when you achieve it? Focus on as many details as possible: what do you see, hear, sense, feel, touch, smell, taste? Be as descriptive as possible in your mind to create the most crystal-clear picture that you can.

I've been implementing this strategy for decades, and on top of implementing it – let's say it, having lots of fun doing so – I knew when I was developing my achievement framework that this was a crucial success element as part of the *Lead Beyond The Edge* path. Remember our special ingredient of repetition? So I'd like you to do this again and again and again. I know this is going to be easy, as not only does playing this picture over and over to yourself help with the repetition factor, but seeing yourself having achieved your goal in your mind makes your brain believe that you've actually done it. As a result, your brain will flood with an amazing cocktail of neurochemicals that in turn will make you feel good, give you that extra boost and drive you to make it happen. So it's a real win–win!

I have dozens and dozens of stories where I've seen this happen for me and my clients, and I will always continue to lead beyond the edge and activate my ADOPT circuit, as I will never get bored with feeling so good, getting that amazing sense of achievement, and experiencing these déjà vu moments again and again and again!

This strategy is enabling you to step up your game by boosting your motivation, sustaining your momentum and inspiring you to push through. I did tell you this was the best way to adopt, right? Without our newly built *Adopt* circuit, it is easy for our brain to feel the fear and have you contract and fall back.

But that's not you now, right? You know better than letting your brain stop you in your tracks; now that you have taken it upon yourself to build the missing bookmark, your brain will happily – ah, those great chemical releases! – lead you on this new path of adoption.

This is where you are ready to say:

'I absolutely understand the importance of adoption, and I adopt. By adopting, I'm helping my brain embrace the situation. I understand that by befriending my fear, turning it around into excitement, I create the bookmark that my brain needs to have in order to bring me closer to my goal.'

This new attitude that you have formed is inspiring, and will support you again and again and again on your way to extraordinary results as you lead beyond the edge.

INTRO WIRES

INSPIRING RESILIENCE

You have now continued to set the stage as you have prepared the ground of your mind by building the overarching *Adopt* wire of the second *Lead Beyond The Edge* circuit, using your brain ability to change and create new pathways. Again here, this is a wire that, with repetition, you will strengthen more and more.

For now, it is time to support you even further by focusing on the second part of the full circuit name: *Adopt* ***with Inspiring Resilience.*** You've already done the work for the *Adopt* part and now we continue our path on this journey of achievement by forming the *Inspiring Resilience* wires, thus learning how to overcome adversity.

I decided to name this part of the circuit *Inspiring Resilience* as we can navigate through the challenges in our personal and professional lives. I believe that *Inspiring Resilience* is a key leadership success trait. It helps us adopt the attitude to mindfully push through when things happen around us: at work, when we face high turnover, organizational changes, mergers, interpersonal conflicts; at home, with financial hardship, losses, illnesses…

As a leader – leading yourself, your team, your organization – when you demonstrate resilience, you not only move forward but you also inspire others around you. Thriving in the face of adversity is inspiring. This is leading: first for yourself as you build this part of the path in your brain and second as a ripple effect for others, as you inspire them on their own path. This inspiring shift from setbacks to growth leads you up a fruitful path: a path to success.

Again, to deliver on my promise that the framework is about providing you with all the strategies you need as challenges arise, I'm going to equip you with 3 actionable strategies as you build these 3 new wires, so you can activate these whenever you need them. This is the challenge, where *challenges* are the challenge. This is key because unless you know how to deal with adversity, your goal-reaching journey will come to an abrupt stop right there.

I've personally had my fair share of adversity, and professionally I've been helping clients deal with theirs too as part of my business for years now. I'm not saying that challenges will always come up during your goal journey, but I certainly want to make sure that *should* they come up – because life happens, really – you have it in you to push through no matter what.

Adversity wins when you let it win by giving up and falling back to the middle of your comfort zone. Thanks to these wires, you are going to learn how to inspiringly deal with and overcome it to move forward beyond the edge and reach your goals. This is where you can take charge and build your INSPIRING RESILIENCE wires, so that you can direct your brain to go up the path YOU lead it to!

Once upon a time

Story

'Being bullied by my boss...'

'Hey, you're home! How was your day, my love?' Thinking back about my day, I looked at my husband's face and I found myself unable to articulate any response. His warm and thoughtful welcome as I arrived home and his question about my day made me burst into tears.

I had thought this was a great job at a great company. I had given it my all since the very first day. Having been made redundant at my previous company when it closed, I was thankful to have this great opportunity to bounce back. But no, this was not great at all; in fact, this was a nightmare I was living, day after day.

My boss was bullying me. I could not understand how someone could do that to another person, particularly in a work environment. How could that situation have happened? Why was this happening to me? By then, my husband was tenderly embracing me and holding me in a tight hug as I kept sobbing. I stopped, looked up and said: 'Mon amour, I don't know if I can go on...'

Things happen – happened; are happening; and will happen. This is life with its twists and turns. It is not a pessimistic way of looking at things. By now you know that 'pessimistic' is the last word to come to mind when describing me. I understand why people hope they will never have to face adversity: it is because they fear it. But adversity is part of our life, our career, our organization.

You know what I'm talking about, right? I'm sure that you can think of a challenge that has come up for you before, stopping you in your tracks as you moved towards one of your goals. I'm writing this in the middle of a pandemic. And you might be reading this still in the middle of a pandemic. It happens to all of us: that time, when you feel on track and everything is going great, ticking along and your goal is getting closer, and then BANG, something happens.

I want to be an open book; I believe in creating a genuine and authentic relationship with you. All the stories in this book belong to me. Whether or not we already know each other, one thing for sure is that you know I smile a lot (and yes, that's where my Twitter handle comes from, @IrishSmiley). A client of mine once wrote me a testimonial that started with '*Do not be fooled by the fabulous smile – this is serious work with seriously good results!*' So yes, I do smile a lot, but it does not take away from the challenges I've faced as a child, a teenager and an adult.

Over the years, I've learned to accept adversity, which leads to me overcoming it, as I build and strengthen my resilience, so that no matter what comes up, I continue to make it happen. You have it in you too. An adverse situation does not have power over you, unless you let it have power over you.

The word 'resilience' itself gives us the clue as of the direction we need to lead to thrive. It comes from the Latin word *resilire*, which means to spring back. It is never about having one of those days, but always about controlling one of these moments. Learning how to strengthen your resilience is a positive capacity, and one I know you are ready to dive into so that you can bounce back and forward.

Thanks to the 3 actionable strategies you are about to discover and learn how to implement now, this is exactly what we are going to do: turn adversity on its head, build this resilient capacity of yours and strengthen it. By using the power of your mind to rewire your brain, you form this series of 3 wires and learn how to move from 'Do I have it?' to 'I CAN-DO it!', which is an important success point on your goal-reaching journey.

WIRE 2.1

INSPIRING RESILIENCE – STRATEGY: FRAME

This is where we are building the first of the 3 *Inspiring Resilience* wires as part of your *Adopt with Inspiring Resilience* circuit. As you can see from the highlighted part of this circuit framework in Illustration 9, this is the *Inspiring Resilience – Frame* wire on your path.

2.1

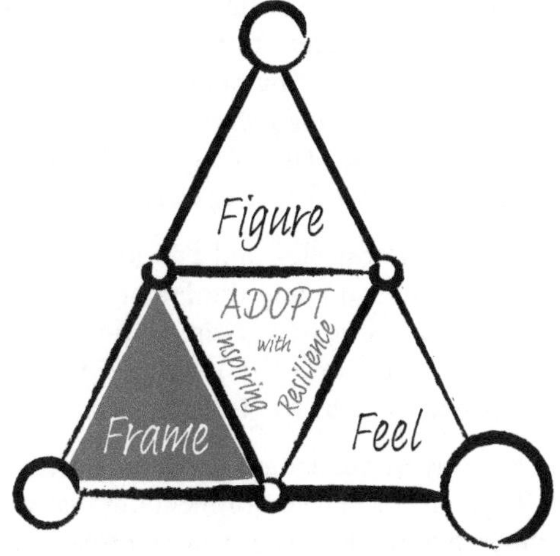

Illustration 9: The *Lead Beyond The Edge* Inspiring Resilience – Frame Wire framework

The language we use is critical, as it builds our reality. Our next wire focuses on teaching you how to retrain your brain to step into the right frame of mind for you to get extraordinary results – the right one is the one that will be most supportive of you achieving your goals, no matter what happens along the way.

So, a challenge arises and…

FRAME!

And yes, before you ask, this is the first of the 3Fs wire strategies we are going to cover within this circuit you are building – again, here I'm using a mnemonic device, a pattern of the letter F, to improve your ability to remember this content.

As a change management consultant, paying attention to my language while communicating to the various departments throughout an organization has always been central. Our choice of words impacts our results. And when announcing a change, which will initially be seen as an obstacle, frames and framing as well as reframes and reframing are key.

By applying this strategy, you learn how to thrive on obstacles. And yes, I know what I just wrote, and I'm pretty sure you had a reaction along these lines: *'Really, "thrive" on obstacles? How am I supposed to thrive on obstacles when everything around me is going wrong and I'm barely keeping up?'* I hear you. This is usually the dialogue that my clients share with me when we first start working together.

It *is* possible to thrive on obstacles, and I'm going to show you how to do exactly that, so you can apply the Frame strategy and activate the wire whenever you need to, so you can continue to move forward. Overcoming adversity starts with the word you use to describe *the what* that has happened to make you feel off track.

I said that the key was in our language, so let's focus on the word 'obstacle'. How do you feel when you think about that word? Probably as if it is something that stands in your way, right? Something that was not meant to be there, yet it is there, and it is stopping you. No wonder your brain resists it then.

What if we reframe the word and its positioning? And I've been doing this throughout, so you've probably picked up on it, whether consciously or unconsciously. Let's reframe the word 'obstacle' with the word 'challenge'. A challenge brings on the idea of a dare, where you want to say: *'A challenge, I hear? Bring it on!'* It is a lot easier to embrace and rise up to a challenge than it is an obstacle.

An obstacle is like a barrier, which makes it difficult to pass through; it is discouraging and not conducive to action. Whereas a challenge is like a fence: you can see through it and it gives you hope to pass through. Think about it: it is a lot more appealing to join a 30-day challenge than a 30-day obstacle, right? A challenge enthuses your brain. That is the power of the shift.

Continuing to pay attention to our language, you know this proverb, right? *'Every cloud has a silver lining.'* Do you remember, as a child, lying on the grass, looking up at the clouds? At first a cloud is just a cloud, but by focusing you were suddenly able to see a particular shape. This is another way of thinking of your frames. Here, you focused on a cloud, the frame, and cognitively reframed it, to then see it as an animal for instance.

This is how this actionable strategy works. You have it in you to focus on the frame and then do a reframe. It instantly changes it in your mind and subsequently, instils a very different set of reactions, which is where we want to be when we are facing adversity. I agree that some situations and events are out of your control, but you *do* control your reactions, and letting these impact you is your choice.

Science

Albert Einstein said, *'No problem can be solved from the same level of consciousness that created it.'* And this aligns very nicely with what we've learned so far about focusing on the frame and applying the right reframe to help you continue to make it happen. When adversity strikes, it creates a problem. So now read that quote again. Thanks to your reframe, you are able to access a different level of consciousness.

Scientifically, this strategy is referred to as *cognitive reframing*. It includes cognitive flexibility and cognitive reappraisal. Cognitive reframing comes from the work of Aaron T. Beck in the 1960s – he is a psychiatrist, known for fathering cognitive therapy as well as cognitive behavioural therapy (CBT).

Cognitive reframing is an emotion-regulation strategy primarily associated with resilience, and its effectiveness has been proven again and again via studies. More recently, neuroimaging studies have shown that cognitive reframing stimulates the activity in the thought control regions of the brain while decreasing the activity in the emotion centre of the brain.

James J. Gross (2002), a psychologist known for his work in emotion regulation, says, *'Reframing has emerged as a really strong form of emotion regulation, and one that's associated with a range of good outcomes.*

People who practice it report less anxiety, less depression, and better social connections.'

Changing the negative thought that triggers the negative emotion enables you to regulate your emotions. This strategy shifts control over to you thanks to your ability to influence how you experience the situation. By changing the frame – that is, the meaning of the situation – you are changing its narrative. This leads you to thinking, feeling and acting differently.

This strategy gives you the ability to shift how you view things, finding a different and more positive interpretation of the adverse situation, thus impacting your next move. I encourage you to activate this wire as often as you need to. You may have heard of some people referring to resilience as a muscle; while scientifically it is not, they are in fact referring to the fact that the more you activate the wire, the easier it gets to fire it up. It is a neural pathway – one that you can actively strengthen.

Linking back to the power of being self-aware, this strategy relies on you doing a conscious shift. It is a commitment and a personal responsibility. You know how all these strategies are close to my heart and brain, and this one in particular has served me and continues to serve me again and again. I believe it is due to its amazing ability to turn adversity on its head.

The more you use this wire, the more it opens up your world of opportunities. Opportunities to change. Opportunities to grow. Opportunities to lead. Obstacles and problems can often be thought of as static. Challenges and opportunities can be experienced as exciting. It engages your competitive spirit, thus motivating and driving you.

Cognitive reframing helps you shift how you look at something, appreciating different aspects of it. It is about looking at things differently, which therefore helps you to adapt your reactions to it. As leaders, this is an extremely useful and empowering strategy, as it gives you the ability to reinterpret any situations that come your way. Plus, remember the way you respond to adversity not only impacts you but also others in your life, at work and at home: by leading yourself, you lead your team and your organization.

And here you go: you now have this FRAME strategy that you can use whenever you need to. You can apply it for any of your goals as this *adversity* challenge comes up for you. Next, the '2.2' wire strategy within this circuit…!

WIRE 2.2

INSPIRING RESILIENCE – STRATEGY: FEEL

This is where we are building the second of the 3 *Inspiring Resilience* wires as part of your *Adopt with Inspiring Resilience* circuit. As you can see from the highlighted part of this circuit framework in Illustration 10, this is the *Inspiring Resilience – Feel* wire on your path.

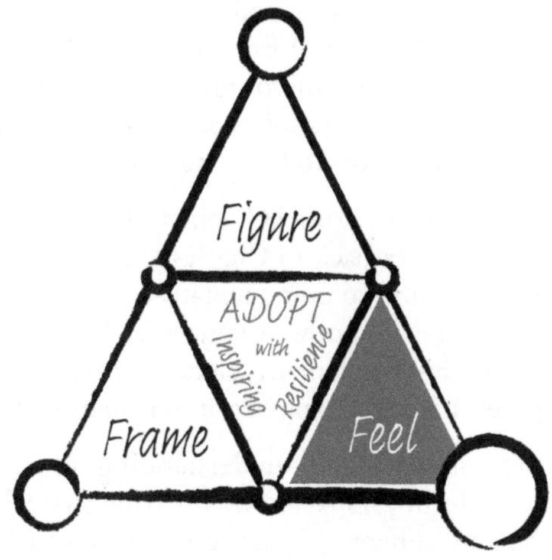

Illustration 10: The *Lead Beyond The Edge* Inspiring Resilience – Feel Wire framework

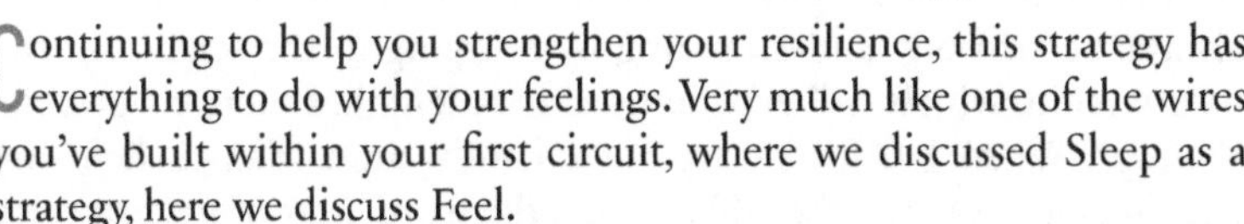

Continuing to help you strengthen your resilience, this strategy has everything to do with your feelings. Very much like one of the wires you've built within your first circuit, where we discussed Sleep as a strategy, here we discuss Feel.

Everybody sleeps and everybody feels, but not everyone does these correctly. Unless managed, your feelings can not only physically impact your body but also control you. Your decisions and actions are driven by your feelings, so they have everything to do with your overall performance and results. Here you are going to learn how to take charge of your feelings to help you manage them better.

So, a challenge arises and…

FEEL!

We do feel, and indeed with adversity, oh yes, we feel, right? Situations and events that pop up in our life make us feel a certain way. This strategy is about helping you raise your awareness about your feelings, which will result in you feeling more resilient towards hardship. It's about gaining control of your feelings so you respond the way you want in any situation.

As you discover this strategy and read words such as 'awareness' and 'feelings', you may be thinking of Emotional Intelligence (EI) – you might have attended a training and/or read a book on the topic before. EI, also referred to as EQ (for Emotional Quotient), is often listed as one of the top leadership traits to have and develop.

While most people think of Daniel Goleman when it comes to EI, we can actually trace its roots back to Charles Darwin and his work on human emotions for survival and adaptation in the late nineteenth century. Here – and this is another example of, how throughout this book, thanks to the advances in neuroscience, we are able to go beyond such construct – we harness the power of our brain to dive deeper.

The key to this strategy is in understanding more about your emotions and your feelings, specifically realizing that while these are intertwined, they are different. It can be confusing when so many people use both these words interchangeably, but that's wrong.

By not understanding their differences and mistakenly using both of these words similarly, you are missing an opportunity that could rob you of the potential to take charge. So, let's differentiate between them now.

In short, emotions are physical while feelings are mental. We will, as always, deepen our understanding by bringing in the science in the next section, which will expand on this at length. Emotions precede Feelings. When I teach this, I use a handy little trick to help my training clients remember their order: the word 'Emotion' starts with the letter E; the word 'Feeling' starts with the letter F. In the alphabet, E comes before F. Emotions precede Feelings.

At its core, this wire strategy comes down to asking yourself the following question: '*Are my feelings supporting or hindering me on my goal journey?*' One great and fun way to find this out is to tune into your body. Indeed, while your feelings are mental experiences, they do accompany a change in your body state.

So how is your body feeling? This series of physiological reactions arises as a result of you having assigned a feeling to your emotion. It is my experience and expertise that unmanaged – often unconscious – feelings do try to communicate with you by clueing you in via your body.

But only if you pay attention; I cannot reiterate it enough that awareness is key. When fear, the emotion, comes up as you are going for your goal and getting close to the edge, wanting to step out of your comfort zone, it is common to experience these: '*This feels like I've butterflies in my tummy.*' '*This feels like a knot in my stomach.*' '*This feels like I have dark clouds above my head.*' '*This feels like I have the weight of the world on my shoulders.*' See what I mean?

When you find yourself using any or all of these words, pay attention. Just as you are entirely responsible for any of these, you have it in you to identify and change these. Remember, be the boss of your mind. Gaining consciousness of these is the way to get rid of them. The Feel strategy works by identifying your feelings and their physiological reactions, and then changing them by commanding them to stop.

At this stage, I personally like to do some conscious breathing to help ground myself and connect within. So I recommend several rounds of *box breathing* through your nostrils. Start by exhaling, fully letting out all of the air in your lungs. Then inhale for a count of 4, pause for a count of 4, exhale for a count of 4 and pause for a count of 4. That's one round. Repeat 10 to 12 times, which takes about 3 minutes.

You are in charge and you can manage your feelings whenever you activate the Feel wire strategy. The key to managing your emotions is in realizing *you are deciding* what you are feeling: you interpret your emotions into feelings.

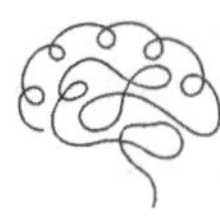

The secret in this control lies in the science, specifically in your brain, as neuroscience shows us where the potential lies. When talking about this, I simply must introduce you to a neuroscientist by the name of Antonio Damasio. His main field is neurobiology, where his research specializes in the neural systems that underlie emotion, decision-making, memory, language and consciousness.

When reading one of his books, which I have, of course, included in the *References* section, I stumbled upon this quote of his. It is very much aligned with what I believe in, as well as how I've been teaching you, so it is a perfect fit within this resilient circuit: '*Scientific knowledge can be a pillar to help humans endure and prevail*' (Damasio 1994).

It sure can, so let's define emotions and feelings to learn even more and strengthen our second wire. Antonio Damasio (in Pontin 2014) says that, '*Feelings are mental experiences of body states, which arise as the brain interprets emotions, themselves physical states arising from the body's responses to external stimuli.*'

Your emotions are made of internal experiences and involve chemical releases throughout the brain and body, while your feelings are your perception of these internal experiences and are very much subjective. This is where the potential lies for you to be empowered because you, involving cognitive input, interpret your emotions into feelings.

On stage, I usually do a little demonstration using a situation that I know my audience members often encounter. Let's do something similar here for you to see, hear and feel what happens when you let yourself be controlled by your feelings and what happens when you control your feelings. So, let's imagine that I am the CMO in a large organization and I've been selected to stand in front of a group to deliver a talk.

Scenario #1: I'm about to stand on stage. I feel that my hands are quite sweaty; my legs are wobbly; my breathing is getting frantic. I'm really nervous. I hear myself say, '*I am really nervous*', and I am nervous. I then start thinking about all of the bad things that could happen.

Now, time out!

Scenario #2: I'm about to stand on stage. I feel that my hands are quite sweaty; my legs are wobbly; my breathing is getting frantic. I think to myself, '*I am excited*', and I'm excited: I'm about to step in front of the group, serve them and rock it. And, I can think of so many ways that I'm going to deliver!

The only difference between those 2 scenarios, which both triggered the threat response, is my interpretation of the same emotion. Two people can interpret the same emotion into 2 very different feelings, impacting their emotional resilience, and thus the results. Chemically speaking, feeling nervous and feeling excited are almost identical.

Did you catch how there was a time out between these 2 scenarios? I have the ideal technique to help you with that. Remember how I provided you with an additional step to our wire strategy by taking you through box breathing? You know by now that there are no coincidences in my writing or my teaching, and here I want to give you some scientific back-up to implementing a breathing technique in your life.

Box breathing can also be called square breathing, tactical breathing, combat breathing or Sama Vritti Pranayama; I initially knew it as the last of these. As a daily yoga practitioner, this is ancient yogic breathing, and I've especially learned how to breathe during my practice and carried it beyond to support me throughout.

This is one of the conscious breathing techniques and you can also use deep slow breathing or alternate nostrils breathing or diaphragmatic breathing. All these breathing techniques are beneficial to your brain. Box breathing recently gained extra popularity as it was shown to be taught to and applied by US Navy SEALs.

Breathing is tied to your nervous system and conscious breathing helps you regulate your autonomic nervous system (ANS) by stimulating the vagus nerve – this nerve, the longest cranial one, runs from your brainstem through the thorax to the abdomen. The ANS has 2 parts: the sympathetic nervous system (SNS), which activates the threat response; and the parasympathetic nervous system (PNS), which activates the relaxation response.

By controlling your breathing, you reset your ANS imbalances as your vagus nerve sends signals to adjust your PNS and your SNS, bringing feelings of calmness and wellbeing throughout your body. It has also been proven to improve your focus and concentration by producing the right amount of *noradrenaline* (a neurotransmitter also called norepinephrine) in your brain.

Do it as you activate this wire, but also experience this technique's effectiveness by doing it at the beginning of your day, before a meeting at work, before delivering a presentation…

This wire strategy activation helps you raise awareness of your emotions and feelings so that you can manage these better, while feeling calm and grounded thanks to your controlled breathing. This conscious breathing gives you the pause you need to appropriately interpret your emotions into feelings, adjusting as necessary and taking deliberate action on your goal path. This is how you build resilience in the face of adversity.

And here you go: you now have this FEEL strategy that you can use whenever you need to. You can apply it for any of your goals as this *adversity* challenge comes up for you. Next, the '2.3' wire strategy within this circuit…!

WIRE 2.3

INSPIRING RESILIENCE – STRATEGY: FIGURE

This is where we are building the third of the 3 *Inspiring Resilience* wires as part of your *Adopt with Inspiring Resilience* circuit. As you can see from the highlighted part of this circuit framework in Illustration 11, this is the *Inspiring Resilience – Figure* wire on your path.

2.3

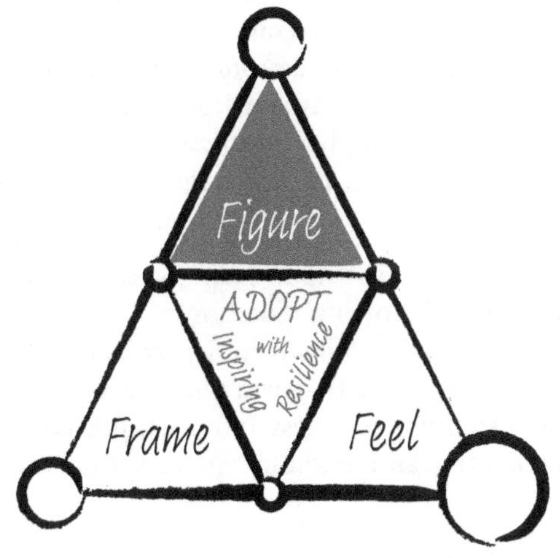

Illustration 11: The *Lead Beyond The Edge* Inspiring Resilience – Figure Wire framework

'*I have not failed. I've just found 10,000 ways that won't work.*' Such wise words from Thomas A. Edison! While some people focus on asking which one of his 1000 inventions, from the incandescent light bulb to the phonograph, led him to say this, I know that you and I will focus on the superb resilience this quote demonstrates.

This brings us to our next and last wire within this circuit: Figure. This actionable strategy may remind you of a process that you have done at work before – indeed, running through a 'Lessons Learned' process is a common practice in a corporate environment, particularly in programme and project management.

I had not realized I was already doing something similar in my life until I was studying for my project management certification and came upon this practice to be implemented towards the end of a project. Over the years, I've certainly facilitated a lot of these sessions with executives, helping them to move forward on a stronger path.

So, a challenge arises and…

FIGURE!

This is again a very straightforward strategy, where you need to figure out what lessons learned you can come up with in the face of adversity. Taking stock and capturing the lesson(s) helps you to figure out the takeaways(s) to carry forward as you learn from your adverse event: it enables you to take strength from these events and resiliently and optimistically move forward. There is something to learn from every experience you have.

It can often be the case that upon facing such an event, you found yourself asking the following questions: *'Why me?', 'Why is this happening to me?', 'Why does this always happen to me?'* It is okay, we've all been there. When you do that, you put your victim hat on. Taking on the role of a victim is a useless and disempowering strategy. You give away your control, and this holds you back from progress towards your goal.

To move forward from there, we apply this strategy and we learn. Growth comes from learning. By turning this around, you change your hat from victim to victor, from useless to empowered, now focusing on the takeaway lesson. Think of your frames here too and stop asking these *why* questions, as no useful answers will come up; instead, start asking these *what* questions, which will lead you to useful responses.

Figure it out and shift from 'Why me?' to 'Yes, me!':

- What can I learn from this?
- What can I take away with me?
- What lesson can help me move forward?

This works when applied to any and all events, from the big ones, such as a pandemic or an earthquake, to daily ones, such as your computer crashing and you losing the email you had been working on for hours, your internet being slow, your post being lost, your supplier being delayed, being stuck in traffic, etc.

I was once interviewed by a national radio host, who asked me what I would change in my past if I could. I still remember looking at him across the studio, facing this giant fluffy mic and giving him one of my smiles as I responded: nothing. He appeared taken aback, and of course asked me to elaborate. You see, I would not change a thing as changing any of the things that have happened in my past would change me too.

I believe that all the things that have happened have shaped me into the person I am today. My life to date, including its adversity, has made me into the woman, wife, daughter, sister, aunt, friend, business owner, keynote speaker and leader I am today. You are the one deciding to be disempowered or empowered by the events happening around you: it's your responsibility. Your reactions, decisions and actions in these special moments determine your future. Challenges make us stronger by teaching us lessons we needed to learn to pursue our goals, grow and make a difference.

Looking at reinforcing our wire strategy here, I'd like to share with you one of my favourite sciences *(I know, I know, I love them all, but this one has a special place in my heart – you'll see!)*. I'm talking about positive psychology. It is the right time to introduce it, as the above strategy and the overall circuit of resilience are particularly inspired by its teaching.

Positive psychology was fairly young when I started my psychology studies and by young I mean that the branch had officially been created by Martin Seligman in 1998. It will come as no surprise to you that it felt like a great fit: I LOVED it then and love it today and will continue to love it tomorrow! A business partner once told me after watching me deliver a breakout on the topic that '*I embodied, lived and breathed positive psychology*'.

Martin Seligman, along with Mihaly Csikszentmihalyi (I know… and you just had to read his surname! Imagine having to speak his name while addressing an audience of 2500 corporate executives!), published the branch foundational paper in 2000. You may have heard of Mihaly Csikszentmihalyi too, as he is most influential in the field and his research and breakthroughs with Flow are well known.

In the words of its founder, positive psychology is the scientific study of positive human functioning and flourishing on multiple levels that include the biological, personal, relational, institutional, cultural and global dimensions of life. It studies the optimal human functioning that aims to discover and promote the factors that allow individuals and communities to thrive.

While psychology approaches the field with the '*What's wrong with me?*' question, positive psychology asks, '*What's right with me?*' and '*What makes life most worth living?*' I have to say that positive psychology is not positive thinking and does not deny life's hardships. It does, however, focus on a set of character strengths, seen as our personal power and the source of our growth. See why I was particularly hooked?

In this field, we focus on 4 topics: positive *experiences* (such as happiness, inspiration, joy); positive *traits* (think of resilience, gratitude, optimism); positive *relationships*; and positive *institutions*. While my approach with organizations is multifaceted, using a blend of science, I do use the science of positive psychology a lot when working with clients.

In the workplace, its findings and insights help create an environment where employees can fulfil their potential. Studies have found that human strengths are the keys to productivity, performance, stress, satisfaction, retention, turnover, absenteeism, creativity and morale, to name a few. A strong and happy employee flourishes at work.

Optimism, and the concept of *learned optimism*, strengthens your resilience to break through barriers and overcome the challenges you may face – at work, think of organizational changes, mergers, technology, conflict, workload, budgets, deadlines… Learning how to be optimistic is an important way to help you maximize your life; it reduces your stress and improves your success. Any time you face an adverse event or situation, activate this wire: figure out the takeaway to become more optimistic and thus resilient.

And here you go: you now have this FIGURE strategy that you can use whenever you need to. You can apply it for any of your goals as this *adversity* challenge comes up for you. Next – not a surprise section anymore, as you know what's coming…!

Continuing to be as practical as possible for you, you'll find a working example, so that you can see how these strategies practically work to tackle an *adversity* challenge thanks to its *Lead Beyond The Edge* solutions.

Let's fire it up!

Wire 2.1: Inspiring Resilience – Strategy: Frame

Wire 2.2: Inspiring Resilience – Strategy: Feel

Wire 2.3: Inspiring Resilience – Strategy: Figure

Scenario ▶ Organize your annual company event.

Every year, your organization hosts a large event for its employees. You've been assisting with previous events, and this year you are in charge for the very first time and are very excited to make it happen. You want to do it BUT you are suddenly faced with adversity: the world is experiencing a pandemic and as countries are going into lockdown one after the other, you realize the event cannot happen physically. *'Oh, why is this happening to me?'*

The 2.1 solution

▶ *Activate the FRAME wire strategy.*

Watch out for your language. You notice that you are looking at this pandemic and its lockdown measures as obstacles. FRAME this as a challenge instead. Looking at it from that angle helps you come up with creative ideas to make this happen virtually using technology, and the ideas start flowing. It can actually be quite fun to look at this as a dare, and you find yourself thinking: *'How can I make this work?'*

The 2.2 solution

▶ *Activate the FEEL wire strategy.*

Your emotions are understandably all over the place, but you know it is up to you to decide what you are feeling. As you tune in your awareness, you FEEL. You notice the various physiological reactions in your body, and you gain control of them. Next, you proceed to do several rounds of box breathing to calm down your nervous system. And then, you ask yourself whether your feelings are supporting or hindering you, and you decide to let go of those that hinder you.

The 2.3 solution

▶ *Activate the FIGURE wire strategy.*

First thing first, you move from victim to victor; yes, this is happening around you, and yes, you can deal with it – but not from a place of disempowerment. This helps you go from the useless 'Why' questions to the useful 'What' questions, which leads you to FIGURE your way. You ask yourself: *'What can I learn from this?' 'What lessons can help me move forward?'* You take strength from this situation and, in the process, see your team take your lead, and move forward with you. These takeaway points are helping you to shape the upcoming event in a way you would have never thought of before this challenge presented itself: you are learning from it and making it work. This event edition will be that extra special.

Any and all of these strategies are helping you demonstrate inspiring resilience as you take charge and push through your comfort zone. You are doing it: you are leading beyond the edge, and organizing your annual company event.

You CAN-DO it!

And *voilà*, there you have them: my 3 actionable strategies to help you overcome adversity. If things happen around you, **frame, feel** and **figure** your way to inspiring resilience to reach your 'I CAN-DO it!' success point. Each of these represents one of the *Inspiring Resilience* wires as part of our second circuit, which you've now entirely built!!!

You will find a recap text version of what you've accomplished in the next section. As for now, I know you are expecting me to close a certain story I opened at the beginning of this *Inspiring Resilience* circuit, right? So, where were we? *Here I was, back home after a terrible day at the office, letting the situation have power over me…*

Story

'Being bullied by my boss and standing up for myself!'

Hearing me say those words, 'Mon amour, I don't know if I can go on…' out loud startled me. I stood up straight, shoulders back, wiped my tears away and looked up. I took a few long breaths, concentrating on deep and slow breathing. As my tears stopped and my heart rate settled, I knew this was working: I was feeling in control.

Enough was enough; it was time to frame this entire situation. 'I can-do it,' I thought. 'Of course, I can. I bounced back from redundancy last year, I can bounce back from this bully too!' Realizing how much I had learned about myself this past year, I knew I had it in me to figure out this challenge. It was time to stop asking myself these questions that were bringing me nowhere and instead start thinking of the future.

These words from Eleanor Roosevelt popped into my mind: 'No one can make you feel inferior without your consent.' *So true. I had let this go on. The second I took responsibility, I felt different: strong, optimistic, resilient. All of this happened in a matter of seconds. My husband and I were still standing next to each other. I squeezed his hand and, with sparkles in my eyes, decided this was the last day I'd come home feeling that way, letting the bully run over me. And indeed, this was the last day I did, and the first day of the rest of my career.*

RECAP CIRCUIT 2/3

ADOPT with INSPIRING RESILIENCE

Double WooHoo!

You have now built your second circuit and its 4 wires!!! Once again here – and this time you know what happens in your brain when you do so – this is definitely a cause for celebration as it gets you even closer to extraordinary results. Do it! What's your reward going to be? How creative can you be with it?

You have used the power of your mind to rewire your brain to create your second circuit and its 4 wires as part of your *Lead Beyond The Edge* bold path. Now continue to strengthen it with repetition every time you activate it. With neuroplasticity, the more you do it, the less you'll have to do it!

Here is a recap text version of what you've accomplished.

Let's Fire It ALL Up!

Lead Beyond The Edge, Circuit 2/3

Activate your second circuit
to help you strengthen your attitudes,
overcome adversity and move from…

Do I have it?

ADOPT with Inspiring Resilience

- Overarching Wire 2: Adopt
  - Intro Wires: Inspiring Resilience
    - Wire 2.1: Inspiring Resilience – Strategy: Frame
    - Wire 2.2: Inspiring Resilience – Strategy: Feel
    - Wire 2.3: Inspiring Resilience – Strategy: Figure
- Recap Circuit 2/3: Adopt with Inspiring Resilience

… to

I CAN-DO it!

Multisensory Learning Boosts: Circuit 2/3

We have already covered the power of our olfactory, tactile and auditory senses at the end of the first circuit, so here I know you've got this and I don't need to re-explain the science behind each of these, nor why and how these science-backed strategies work.

Yet I still want to provide you with the instructions as this is your time to pause and consolidate your learning before jumping into the next circuit. So, here are the instructions for you to apply the 3 learning boosts for your second newly built circuit and its wires. At first glance, this second series of *multisensory learning boosts* may appear quite similar; indeed, here again I'm using the same 3 senses.

But upon reading the instructions, you will notice that while the processes are similar (repetition is key to neuroplasticity!), the cues, the kinaesthetic anchor and the visualization are different, as these now apply to this second circuit. The fact that you again have the instructions here makes it easier for you, so you don't have to flip back and forth through the book: we want to continue moving forward on our path to achievement.

Let's continue engaging and boosting your learning using your olfactory sense:

- Pick the same scent you've picked before. This is important, as you are scent training your brain: the same scent will help you cue it again so that you continue strengthening the pathways.
- Smell it (inhale or diffuse) and reflect on this particular circuit and its wires, and their teachings (which have now been stored as memories in your brain) and write down 3 to 5 insights you've gained as you've built your second circuit. Think of the 4 strategies: Adopt + Frame, Feel, Figure; alternate scent and writing – this will lead you to associate the scent you've chosen with your learning.
- Then sleep.
- Enjoy and repeat!

Let's continue engaging and boosting your learning using your tactile sense:

Here your state is *Adopt with Inspiring Resilience* and your stimulus is the second kinaesthetic anchor I've created for you.

- Elicit the desired state. I'm going to give you 2 steps – remember, the stronger your state, the stronger the anchor.
- *First step:* Read out loud the 3 to 5 insights you've compiled as part of our first learning boost. Make sure these start with 'I…' to fully engage with them; this is about eliciting your state, so go beyond reading and perform these to really feel your insights' impact.
- As you do that, it is time to set your second kinaesthetic anchor, the one for this second circuit and its wires. To form it, press the tip of your thumb firmly to the tip of your middle finger (choose the same hand you've picked for the first anchor); press and pulse it a dozen times while reading your notes.
- *Second step:* Recall a time when you had that can-do attitude, when it felt like: 'Yes, I CAN-DO it!' and then you moved forward to achieve your goal – got it? Step into the memory and be as descriptive as possible: What does it feel like? What do you see? Hear? Touch? Maybe even smell and taste? Feel it throughout your body.
- As you do that, repeat your anchor: press firmly the tip of your thumb to the tip of your middle finger; press and pulse it a dozen times while reliving your memory.
- Release your anchor when you feel at your best, when the peak of the intensity is reached.
- (Optional) Play in the background another one of your favourite energizing songs as you create your anchor.

- Test it. To do so, remember you first have to break your state, which I can help you do by asking you a question that's going to get you to think of something else: so tell me, what is the name of your place of birth? Now that the state has been broken, it is time to fire your anchor. Two things can happen: you will either recall that state or just not yet; most anchors need a couple of times to be fully formed, so simply repeat the process.
- Enjoy and repeat!

Let's continue engaging and boosting your learning using your auditory sense:

- Set aside 15 minutes.
- Seat yourself in a comfortable and undisturbed place.
- Have your computer or your phone with you on do-not-disturb, so you can access the second visualization, but make sure you have turned off emails and any social media alerts so that you maximize your experience.
- Listen to it; you don't need to do anything else, as I will guide you to reflect on this second circuit and its wires helping you think back over your learning and reinforce insights you've gained.
- (Optional) If you are like me and some of my clients, you will want to write down some of the thoughts that popped up during this experience, so then, you will need this next step. Capture what came up – thoughts, decisions, actions – to continue leading you on your goal journey.
- Enjoy and repeat!

Continue using these stimuli so you can trigger even more *Lead Beyond The Edge* memories – this time a particular series of insights you gained as you read and built your second circuit and its wires, whenever you decide to do so.

And this wraps up your second circuit, with its **ADOPT** overarching wire and its 3 *Inspiring Resilience* wires, **FRAME**, **FEEL** and **FIGURE**, as part of your *Lead Beyond The Edge* bold path. Next, you are going to discover how to build your third circuit to continue to lead you to extraordinary results.

As for now, I know you are expecting me to close a certain story I opened at the beginning of this ADOPT circuit, right? So, where were we? *Here I was, at the airport, exhausted, wondering whether I should go back home or push through…*

Story

'Stepping up to help a friend and supporting a client!'

Once upon a time

I was lost. It all felt fuzzy, with so much uncertainty. I understood why my brain and body felt threatened and fearful. Many people would have given up and gone back home by then. I could have called the client and said, 'Sorry, the airport is shutting down due to adverse weather and I will not be able to make it to the event.' But that's not me: I feel strongly about doing the right thing, not the easy thing.

I'm not one to follow the easy path. It was time to lead beyond the edge: I had made a commitment. This was my choice and time to be resilient and keep going. I remember saying to myself, 'Frederique, you've got this!' I knew what to do. I needed to adopt my fear and connect with the goal so my fear would not dictate my next step. And so I did. I pictured taking to the stage the very next day. I heard the MC introducing me, I saw the business professionals' faces and then I saw myself deliver my session.

I imagined it all very clearly; while the situation meant that I did not know much about the venue details, I focused on the details I could control. I saw myself in my complete stage outfit: my dress and my heels; how my hair was put up; which shade of lipstick I had on; how my perfume smelt. I heard the song that was playing for the audience thanks to the AV team. I saw myself smile, thank the MC and hop on stage in front of the audience. Giving them my very best, not letting them in on anything that had transpired over the last couple of days, but instead focusing on serving them to the best of my ability.

This felt amazing and I was so excited: there is nothing that I like more than doing what I absolutely love to do and feel I was born to do: giving my all for my client and their audience, helping them move mountains by using the power of their minds to rewire their brains.

And we sure did that! Lori, later on, emailed me a testimonial: 'Frederique Murphy exceeded my expectations for her session "Full Capacity Brain: Solving Complex Problems and Making Solid Decisions Under Pressure" at our European conference. Not only did she dazzle the attendees on stage, but you would have never guessed that she flew in last minute because a colleague couldn't make it. As a planner, I can't fully put into words how thankful I was that she accommodated the last-minute request and rearranged her schedule to support our event. She truly shines on stage and off.'

The irony of the session content, right? The intensity of the whole experience was so high that I know this will be one of those unforgettable speaking engagements. From beginning to end, it was a thrilling adventure, one for the books…!

ACT with IMPACTFUL CONFIDENCE CIRCUIT 3/3

▶ Overarching Wire 3: Act ▶

▶ Intro Wires: Impactful Confidence ▶

▶ Wire 3.1: Impactful Confidence – Strategy: Engage ▶

▶ Wire 3.2: Impactful Confidence – Strategy: Expect ▶

▶ Wire 3.3: Impactful Confidence – Strategy: Encourage ▶

▶ Recap Circuit 3/3: Act with Impactful Confidence ▶

Acting through your fear is what is left for you to do to go beyond the edge of your comfort zone.

You are on the home stretch!

This is where you bring it all together and make it happen.

You have identified your goal, are ready to accomplish it, believe you can, know you have that can-do attitude and you start doing it.

You are at the 'I DO it!' stage.

When I think about this stage, I feel ecstatic. I do because it is the moment when my goal, the one I've been dreaming of and desiring to achieve, is within my reach. I believe I can and no matter what will stand in my way, I will know what to do to keep going and accomplish it. This is invigorating. I am excited. Full of motivation, energy and enthusiasm. This is happening, and I can hardly contain myself thinking about the bright possibilities and future ahead of me.

I know you've been there too, and as you read this, you want to jump in, right? Let's do it! Think back to a goal you've achieved, something you had wanted to do and you did it. Now rewind a bit and find the moment when you believed you could do it and had everything you needed to do so, right before stepping in on the goal journey. Remember how you felt as you were at the edge, full of anticipation, ready to start. What does it feel like? What do you see? Hear? Touch? Maybe even smell and taste? Got it? What a feeling, right?

And then, BANG, something happens: one day, you don't do it and fall off track. You come up with excuses, you procrastinate, you lose momentum. Sounds familiar? It is like you are doubting yourself, wondering whether it's even worthwhile and whether in fact you want to be back on track…

This is where the third circuit comes in as part of your *Lead Beyond The Edge* path: the one where you and I are going to build the series of wires in your brain to create the new neural pathways that are necessary to take you from this 'Can I do it?' stage to our third success point on your journey as you reach your 'I DO it!' stage, which leads you to the exhilarating 'I DID IT!!!' stage.

'We are what we repeatedly do.
Excellence, then, is not an act,
but a habit.' Will Durant

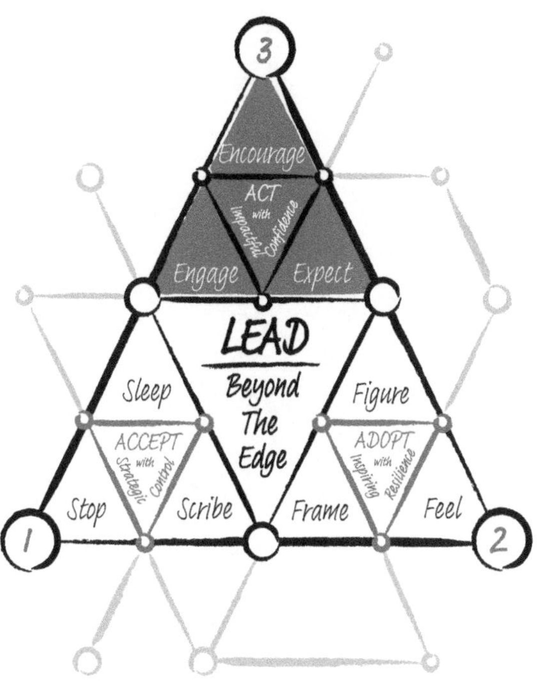

Illustration 12: The *Lead Beyond The Edge* Act with Impactful Confidence Circuit framework

This third circuit has everything to do with your behaviours. You will learn how to convince your brain to do it, as well as understand why you have to do this in the first place, expanding your brain knowledge. You will also know what to do in order to learn how to boost your confidence so it drives your motivation again and again.

Remember, the success key leading you to extraordinary results, in an approach that is both results-driven and mindful, is focusing on that 'I'm doing it' flow. Upon building that third circuit and implementing these 3 actionable strategies, there will be no stopping you in your tracks as you reach your goal!!!

Ready? Let's build it!

From 'Can I do it?' to 'I DO it!' leading you to 'I DID IT!!!'

OVERARCHING WIRE 3

ACT

Story

'Dreaming of writing a book...'

The journalist asked me one last question as he closed our interview: 'So, Frederique, tell me and our readers, what's the next mountain you're moving? What does the future hold for you and your Mountain Movers community? I smiled, laughing softly and thought to myself: 'Oh, how I know exactly what my next big goal is!'

Write a book. This goal was totally aligned with my big vision; just thinking about it made me feel a flurry of happy butterflies in my tummy. This felt right. And it was definitely one of the ways I could continue making a difference and impacting my clients in their organizations and associations.

Truth be told, I had been thinking about it for a while but had not yet made it a priority. This reminded me of when I launched my company. I incorporated it in 2008, but I had been thinking about it for years before that. I believe that everything happens for a reason and that things fall into place when they are meant to, so as long as I kept moving forward, I trusted the process and knew I'd recognize the moment.

And that moment had arrived: I was ready to take that next step and make it happen. So I answered, 'Thanks so much for asking. I'm super excited to share with you and your readers that a book is in my future!!!' This was in March 2018. I remember it clearly as it happens to coincide closely with celebrating my first 10 years in business.

This was the first time I had publicly talked about it, but the shift had happened a few months back as I kept on dreaming more and more about my book. Henry David Thoreau said: 'If you have built castles in the air, your work need not be lost; that is where they should be. Now put the foundations under them.' And, I was ready to do so then.

But by the end of 2019, there was still no book. A lot had happened since that day. I'm resilient, so I continued pushing through. I pushed through a 7.1 magnitude earthquake in central Mexico; I pushed through a debilitating disease; I pushed through a difficult surgery. And there was more. Days passed; weeks passed; months passed. The next thing I knew it had been over a year since I had started this goal of mine, and I had nothing to show for it.

I had fallen off track. I had lost momentum. I started doubting myself. A question ran through my mind: 'Will I ever see my book in airport bookstores? This was important to me: as a keynote speaker, when I travel to my clients' events around the world, I always enjoy seeing my peers and mentors' books in the shops and have dreamed of having mine on the shelf right next to theirs. But at this stage, I was not sure anymore. More questions: 'Is it worth it? 'Am I up to this?', 'Will it ever happen…?'

Strategy

As we continue on this journey of achievement, our third and last circuit is going to be focusing on our behaviours. Let's continue to add to our leading statement we've been building. So far, we have 'everything we want to achieve starts in our brain, ignited and fuelled by our beliefs, supported and influenced by our attitudes', and now we can add, 'brought to fruition by our behaviours'.

So, as we continue this journey, your third mission is going to be to ensure that you consistently do it. It is about building and implementing consistent behaviours that sustain your momentum as you make it happen. This is where you can take charge and build your ACT circuit, so you can continue directing your brain to go up the path YOU lead it to and bring it to completion as you reach your goal!

This is where we are building the third of the 3 *Lead Beyond The Edge* circuits. As you can see from the highlighted part of this circuit framework in Illustration 13, this is the *Act with Impactful Confidence* circuit, and for now we are going to focus on the *Act* part of it and build that overarching wire on your path.

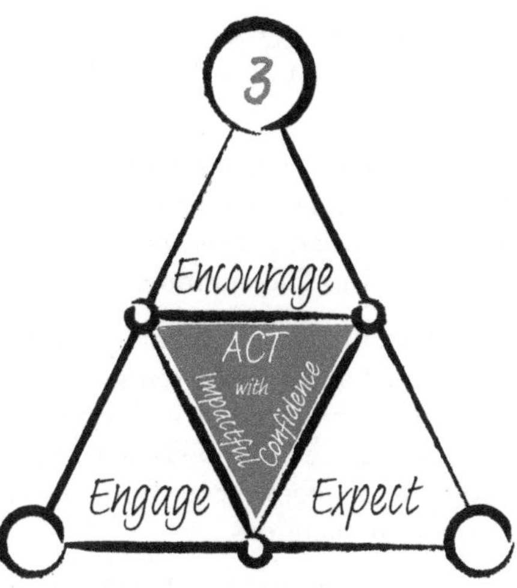

Illustration 13: The *Lead Beyond The Edge* Act Wire framework

Oh yes, our last overarching wire! You and I have been on a journey all right! Together so far, I've led you to accept your fear, then to adopt your fear, and now – if you could see me right now, you would be watching me roll up my sleeves and probably also hear me do a little drumroll sound effect – yes, this is it: our third overarching wire, where *you* are going to act through your fear.

Did the words *'How, how, how...?!?!'* just pop into your mind? I bet you are wondering: *'How do I do that, Frederique?'* probably because what you are actually wondering is, *'Why would I do that, Frederique – sounds scary to me!'* You know I'm going to show you exactly how to do that next step. Out of our 3 overarching wires – Accept, Adopt and now Act – this is the most straightforward one, in the sense that it says it all on the tin.

Acting is the third overarching wire on our bold path.

Acting through your fear is what is left for you to do to go beyond the edge of your comfort zone; it is that step that stands between where you are right now and where you want to be to reach your goal. That in itself should make you feel that extra bit excited, right? Hence, the drumroll...! As you must have picked up, I'm right there with you, and indeed very much excited.

I'm excited because I know that this is about making it all happen, honing in on all of the work you've done up to now: having built 2 of the 3 circuits as part of the *Lead Beyond The Edge* path; having already succeeded in convincing your brain to take you up on a bold new path; and now starting on the third and last circuit, bringing it all together by acting.

From here on, every action you take brings you closer to your goal. Every single one of your actions will reinforce that you are doing it. Come on, say it out loud with me: '*I am doing it!*' And, taking action is all about behaviours. So, let's find out more.

After studying attitudes, my social psychology curriculum moved to behaviours. There I learned that behaviours consist of our external reactions to internal and external stimuli within our environment. And, even more important, that we can modify our behaviours according to positive or negative reinforcements from our environment or according to self-directed intentions.

Remember how in the *Introduction* I shared with you my passion for human behaviour? Still to this day, it fascinates me. I'm sure you know by now that I'm not much of a passive person, so I actively started looking into it then (and now!). That brought me to studying Behaviour Change and using Organizational Behaviour Management principles to improve the organizational performance of leaders within their organizations. Because that is where the potential lies: in the change. And in your brain, in its plasticity, like we've been demonstrating as you have been forming new wires.

Our beliefs and attitudes guide and affect our behaviours (and yes, that's why we covered these as part of our first 2 circuits!). So now we're bringing it back to our next move, which is to act. At this stage, you are very close to the walls of your comfort zone. I often imagine myself in my zone at this stage, and I can see myself right at the wall, with both of my hands up against it, fingers stretched out. And as I push with my hands, the wall expands and I'm able to take my first step beyond.

This is where you are too. You've learned so much already and by doing the work and building your path, you went from sitting in the middle of your comfort zone, where you used to passively think of what was outside, to now actively taking a stand, literally by the wall. You are ready to push through your fear and take action. And that's amazing!

I know you are ready because your goal, now being right beyond the edge, is within your reach. And when something is so clear in front of us, we feel it all over. This surge of energy and enthusiasm: smiling broadly, eyes sparkling, fingers tingling. You are motivated.

You know that feeling, when this happens and you are motivated to act? It's a wonderful feeling, isn't it? It is one that we would love to hold on to forever! What if you could? Your brain holds the answer and I'm certainly going to give it to you as we build this *Act* overarching wire, so you can make this happen again and again and again.

When I think of motivation, an extra-wide smile appears on my face and I think of these words from Zig Ziglar: '*People often say motivation doesn't last. Neither does bathing – that's why we recommend it daily.*' I was privileged to hear it spoken from stage by the man itself, at an event we both spoke at in 2010, in Dallas, Texas. Sharing the stage with one of the greatest pioneers in the personal development field was a dream come true.

I especially love teaching this part (I know, another one!). I love it because it helps move you from that moment right before the edge to that moment when you are doing it – that moment when you are motivated and take that step beyond. See what I mean? This is exciting: this is the first day of the rest of your life!

Thanks to your acting behaviour, you are dynamically on your way to leading beyond the edge. On your way to achieving every single one of your goals, to be, do and have everything that you desire. On your way to making it happen. Do it: break through the wall of your comfort zone. This excitement is firing up your brain, and it sure is ready to follow your lead beyond the edge, and ACT.

This new behaviour of yours of acting through the fear gives you the upper hand over your brain as you help it cheer you on. Talking about helping you, let's add the science behind it so I can continue to increase your awareness, and at the same time reinforce this new behaviour of yours. Once the science is fully laid out, you'll be totally convinced how pushing through with action is your way to success.

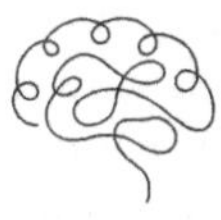

I briefly mentioned motivation as we were building the second overarching wire – when we spoke about visualizing the achieved goal – as this strategy does result in boosting your motivation. Here, we are going to discover the ins and outs of it, the science of motivation, so you can learn how to get and stay motivated and never have to wait for it to show up.

Most people believe they have to wait for motivation and then they will be ready to act. But I know that you and I are different. First, we certainly do not wait on things we know we can activate ourselves as this would take our power away; and second – are you ready for this? – I love it: motivation is not what triggers behaviour; behaviour is what triggers motivation. And beyond that drive, behaviours trigger a wonderful process in your brain, whereby it suddenly turns around, notices what you are up to and activates an incredible and fascinating feedback loop.

So, motivation… It is all in your head! I've been wanting to say that for a while, and it is a great fit here, so here you go, I had to. It sure is all in your head. How exciting to know that there is a way for you to stimulate motivation in your brain. At this stage of your journey towards your goal – strengthening the ACT wire you are building as part of your third and last circuit – your next step towards extraordinary results is to take action, and when you do that, your brain will not only support you and your goals, but also cheer you on, for you to achieve them one after another after another, by motivating you to act and act and act again. I'm passionate about science – here, neuroscience – as it helps us to achieve our extraordinary.

I want to share with you what I've coined the 'I A.M.' process, where A.M. stands for Action and, you've guessed it, M stands for Motivation. Thanks to this handy mnemonic, you will always remember the order in which these happen: Action precedes Motivation. Remember how I said that the other way around takes your power away? The key is not to wait for something to passively show up, but instead actively make it happen: taking action is fully within your control. You control whether or not you act. Without action, there is no success.

At that moment, when you activate your *Act* overarching wire and take action to lead beyond the edge, that next step is as simple as a snap of your fingers. It leads you to progressing and that progress raises up your anticipation of what's to come, and your brain activates the *reward system.* We've talked about threat and with everything we've learned so far, you know how much duality there is in our brain, so now it is time to talk about reward.

The reward system, a group of neural structures in our brain, is a circuit that causes feelings of pleasure when it is activated by something we enjoy — it can also be activated by impulses for drugs, alcohol and gambling, triggering addiction, but here we are focusing on the positive benefits of the system as it helps us with our behaviours and results.

The reward system was originally discovered accidently by 2 neurologists by the names of Peter Milner and James Olds in 1954. It is the way your brain helps you notice something that is important to you, then learns from it so it can help you repeat it. This reinforces behaviour associated with reward. There are several reward pathways in the brain.

Here we are going to concentrate on the one called the *mesolimbic dopaminergic pathway*, the brain areas that control behaviour and memory. This pathway connects the ventral tegmental area (VTA), where neurons release dopamine, to the ventral striatum of the basal ganglia.

This is where the system kicks in as a feedback loop as your brain learns which activity brings you pleasure, so the next time you can even more easily repeat the behaviour. This is what I mean when I said the brain supports and cheers you on as you take action and get closer to your goal. Your brain triggers the motivation for you to achieve your goal.

An important key here to remember is that, as a result of the reward system activating, your brain releases dopamine. In neurochemistry – which studies the chemical basis of nerve and brain activity – we learn that neurochemicals are chemical substances involved in neural activity: think of neurotransmitters, hormones and neuromodulators.

Dopamine is a neurotransmitter and you might have heard that it is linked to pleasure. That is true, but it does more. Scientific studies have proven how it is also deeply linked to motivation, and what we call *motivational salience* – it is a cognitive process that motivates your behaviours towards or away from an outcome; that 'want' attribute towards the attractive form is called *incentive salience*. The reward induces *appetitive behaviour*.

Now, even if it is the first time you've heard about dopamine, I know you've experienced its effect before. You know that feeling you get when you know you are progressing towards your goal because you've just taken a step towards it, that excitement and satisfaction you feel as you get closer and closer and start seeing your goal more and more clearly? Feels familiar, right? Thank your brain – it is the dopamine at play.

Once the dopamine is released, you feel good and you want more, so you keep on going. The release inspires you to act, so you get to the pleasurable reward again and again. Dopamine increases your pleasure and your behaviours. Anticipation triggers it. It is a powerful feedback loop that repeats as long as you continue activating it – and why would you stop when you get reward after reward? You learn that your actions result in rewards and you are motivated to repeat it, so you can get more. This is what we call *self-directed learning*.

Nothing will beat taking that step and I know you know what it leads you to, so you are doing it. But what about if you need a little push? Thanks to more studies on this topic, we've learned that there are ways for you to release dopamine – what a power you have, no wonder I've been saying that you and your brain are amazing!

Here are my 3 go-to dopamine power buttons:

1. Listen to your favourite music.
2. Do an aerobic exercise (it must get your heart rate up).
3. Strike things through or tick them off a list.
   (This one is particularly known in our home; I'm going to make you laugh and maybe you'll relate too: I love the surge of dopamine so much that I've been known to write some items on my list that I have already completed, so I could get my dopamine hit by striking them through!).

So only 2 simple questions remain. Think of your goal and ask yourself:

1. What is my next step?
2. What reward am I going to get?

Both answers to these can be anything. In my BIG goal of making a difference, thinking about my business and how I am so passionate about helping leaders lead extraordinarily, my next step could be to tell you, as you are reading and learning from me right now, that if you know of an organization or an association that could benefit from this material, please do reach out to me – and *voilà*! This next step fits right in: it is small, yet aligned and impactful, and it has the potential to drive great opportunities. As for my reward, you know me, so the pure idea that I could work with you and help you do more already gives me a hit, but on top of that I will go and enjoy some me-time and practise yoga. This is me doing it.

So, what are your next 2 'I A.M. doing it' strategy moves? One step; one reward. Have fun and be creative for the reward. I once hosted a livestream for my community to celebrate reaching a 100th milestone and gave 100 reward ideas – it was a lot of fun! I still remember where I shot it from and as I was going through the list, the anticipation was building up like crazy in my brain – I mean, think about it, 100 rewards, and I was physically surging, very much like what I get from being on stage.

Got yours? Then you are all set, and it is time to activate your newly built *Act* circuit, take action and get your reward. That first step is often the scariest, and yet you must take it to obtain something different. Without it, it is all too easy for your brain to tick along, not lead you beyond the edge and stay inside your comfort zone. But not you: this overarching wire helps you continue that momentum you want to experience. This strategy gives you the one thing you can do to make it all happen: take action. And as it happens, you are driven to make even more happen – this is the positive feedback loop that you've entered.

As leaders, this impacts us, but also think of the impact it can have for the people around you: at work, your team members, colleagues, clients and suppliers; at home, your family and friends. Now you've learned how to elicit a reward reaction for yourself and the people you lead, you know how to maximize productivity and engagement. And remember the importance of happiness? There's nothing like rewards to make people happy.

This is where you are ready to say:

> *'I absolutely understand the importance of action, and I act. By acting, I'm helping my brain cheer me on. I understand that by pushing through my fear, taking that next step, I signal to my brain that this next step is important to me, thus I get rewarded for it, and continue that all the way till I reach my goal.'*

This new behaviour that you have formed is an impactful behaviour, which will support you again and again and again on your way to extraordinary results as you lead beyond the edge.

INTRO WIRES

IMPACTFUL CONFIDENCE

You have now continued to set the stage as you have prepared the grounds of your mind by building the overarching *Act* wire of the third *Lead Beyond The Edge* circuit, using your brain's ability to change and create new pathways. Again here, this is a wire that, with repetition, you will strengthen more and more.

For now, it is time to support you even further by focusing on the second part of the full circuit name: *Act* ***with Impactful Confidence.*** You've already done the work for the *Act* part and now we continue our path on this journey of achievement by forming the *Impactful Confidence* wires, thus learning how to stop procrastination.

I decided to name this part of the circuit *Impactful Confidence* as we can powerfully progress towards our goals with our ability to do so. I believe that *Impactful Confidence* is a key leadership success trait. A lack of confidence takes you on a disappointing and demotivating path. Leadership always starts from within, and leading confidently not only impacts you but also others around you: at work, with your colleagues and team members; at home, with your family and friends.

Confidence guides us to act and behave both consistently and mindfully on our journey. It also helps us avoid putting off tasks, and instead align our actions for maximum results. It drives you and others to impactful behaviours, such as the ability to empower, motivate, inspire, decide, innovate... It leads you to a much richer path.

As I'm continuing to deliver on my promise that the framework is about providing you with all of the strategies you need as challenges arise, I'm going to now equip you with 3 actionable strategies as you build these 3 new wires, so you can activate these whenever you need them.

Confidence is a challenge as long as you believe you either have it or don't. Without it, reaching your goals is hard, as your confidence impacts your courage to act, and thus your success. This is a topic very close to my heart; thinking back on my old self, I'm a bit fidgety. I think the best way to describe me back then was that I was a shadow of myself. Saying that I was not confident was an understatement and it crippled me in all areas of my life.

But then I learned that confidence is not innate. It is not something you are born with or without; you can acquire it at any point in time, so that you can confidently approach the wall of your comfort zone and proudly lead beyond the edge and reach your goals. This is where you can take charge and build your IMPACTFUL CONFIDENCE wires, so that you can direct your brain to go up the path YOU lead it to!

Story — Once upon a time

'Getting assigned to a special project...'

Grand-Père had asked me to meet him in the library at 9 am. As I walked in, a few minutes before – he had taught me that punctuality was really important and a sign of respect – I was taken aback: I'm sure my surprised face said it all!

I must have been 9 or 10 years old and I had never seen anything like it. All the books had been taken off the shelves. There were piles and piles of books on the floor – so many piles and some of them taller than me. With a confused expression, I looked up at him. He explained that he had a special mission for me: I was to sort and catalogue all the books.

Completely shocked, I tried to respond but felt speechless. The magnitude of the project completely overwhelmed me. I finally managed to say with a quiver in my voice: 'But how can I do it?' With a mysterious look on his face, he smiled at me and said he knew I could, then he exited the room. Left by myself, I sat on the ground among all of the books, feeling deflated.

There are times in our life when we feel stuck and unable to move, full of doubts and insecurities, and then BANG, our confidence shakes and negatively impacts our next move. This lack of confidence leads us to action inertia, which is directly counterproductive to doing it as we accomplish our goals.

Let's dive in and discover more about confidence. You know how much I love linguistics, right? And here this scientific study of language delivers again! Did you know that the word 'confidence' comes from the Latin word *cōnfidentia*, where *cōnfidō* means believe, *con* means with and *fidō* means trust. This gives us such a straightforward definition of the word: believe with trust. This is strong, so I'll use a strong word. Confidence is the conviction you have in yourself, and your skills and abilities.

Working with clients on this, I hear a lot of excuses for why some people lack confidence and how, because of such and such, they cannot be confident. The top 2 traits that are often listed and incorrectly considered to result in low confidence are shyness and introversion. Being shy and/or being introverted are 2 personality traits that do not hold you back from confidence. I know this intimately: *'Hi, my name is Frederique, and I'm a shy, introverted and confident woman!'*

As leaders, confidence is an impactful asset: it drives, it influences, it projects, it attracts. I believe confidence is a state of mind – where we think confidently, feel confidently and act confidently. A state of mind that we can consciously step into every single day. Confident people are not born with it; they don't *just* have it: we have it because we know how to turn it on.

On top of the 3 actionable strategies we are going to learn to rewire your brain for confidence, I'd like to give you an additional strategy that you can use right now and thereafter anytime you feel the need to. It is a powerful confidence boost and it will only take you 2 minutes. I've personally been doing it for years and was thrilled when it was backed by science thanks to the persistent work of Amy Cuddy, a social psychologist.

I'm also sharing this particular strategy with you to demonstrate the drive and determination of this team of scientists. They continued to act and push through after originally receiving some harsh criticism and having to do more work to be able to claim that power-posing is indeed science, which they did with ample evidence. So let's do it. Read it first and then put the book down, stand up and do it. It is pretty easy, really: think of Wonder Woman or Superman and imitate their power pose, hold it for 2 minutes and feel that confidence injection!

Having the ability to move through life, through your career, through your organization with confidence allows you to avoid action inertia, thus confidently moving towards your extraordinary as you accomplish your goals. Let's do it and together learn how to boost that confidence of yours. By forming this series of 3 wires in your brain, you learn how to move from 'Can I do it?' to 'I DO it!', which is an important success point on your goal-reaching journey, as it is the penultimate one before reaching the exhilarating 'I DID IT!!!' stage as you achieve it.

WIRE 3.1

IMPACTFUL CONFIDENCE – STRATEGY: ENGAGE

This is where we are building the first of the 3 *Impactful Confidence* wires as part of your *Act with Impactful Confidence* circuit. As you can see from the highlighted part of this circuit framework in Illustration 14, this is the *Impactful Confidence – Engage* wire on your path.

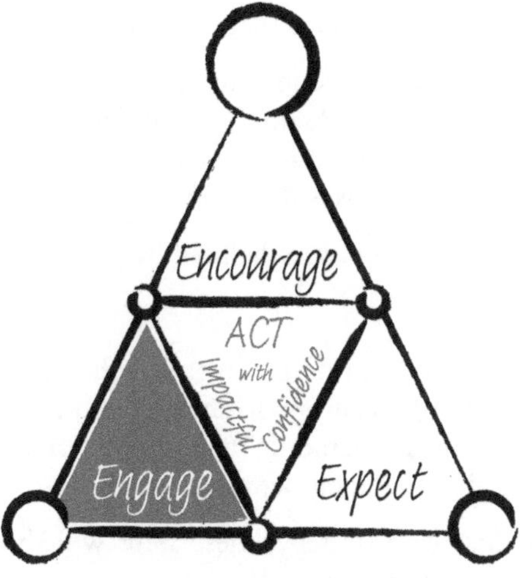

Illustration 14: The *Lead Beyond The Edge* Impactful Confidence – Engage Wire framework

I know this challenge can be a frustrating phase, and that frustration is good because it shows you care. If you were not frustrated, then it would be a different kettle of fish, as you'd need to go all the way back to your opening goal statement: 'I want to do it' because something would have changed there. But not you. This is frustrating because here you are: you want to achieve something, you believe you can, you have that can-do attitude, but yet you are not taking action.

Yes, it is that P word: you are procrastinating. This is such a hot topic and with over 50 million internet search hits, it is something that is faced a lot. Procrastination is one of the ways we self-sabotage. It is an extremely harmful behaviour: on a short-term basis, disruptive; and on a long-term basis, destructive.

Being so results-driven myself, this is something I'm very aware of when it happens to me, and with these 3 wires strategies, we are going to look at confidently taking action by tackling the root cause of procrastination. There is always a reason for this behaviour, and I believe that with a strong set of strategies you can learn how to stop it before it even starts. So, instead of activating this wire when you feel uncertain and confused about what's next, you activate this wire right from the get-go: the difference is that you bypass the frustration phase.

This first strategy covers action inertia due to uncertainty and confusion. Remember when I said that confidence was a state of mind, one that we can step into by thinking confidently, feeling confidently and acting confidently? This is the *think* component.

So, when you find yourself overwhelmed by your goal…

ENGAGE!

And I know you were waiting for it: this is the first of the 3Es wire strategies we are going to cover within this circuit you are building – again here, I'm using a mnemonic device, a pattern of the letter E, to improve your ability to remember this content.

Engage is our first wire strategy; these steps will show you how to confidently engage with your goal:

1. *Spend time on your plan of action for your goal.* The idea here is to increase your awareness of the clear and aligned next steps ahead. I'm adding the word 'next' here as planning is key, but it does not mean to overplan and know step #486…! I've seen so many people freeze before even starting, feeling stuck by a multi-multi-multi-row action plan table. Confidently map out your steps, goals and milestones. Focus on knowing where you are right now, where you are going and what needs to be done to lead in that direction. Remember what it takes to get the ball rolling: that one first action. So focus on the first step and drive momentum. In the words of Martin Luther King Jr,

'You don't have to see the whole staircase, just take the first step.' Planning helps you engage better as it makes your goal more actionable.

2. *Break your goal into a series of chunks.* In order to avoid feeling overwhelmed by one of your goals, which can be paralyzing, this step helps you take your big goal and chunk it down into smaller, specific and manageable steps. These steps take the fear out of the big 'how' question too. Focusing on a chunk and then another one and then another one helps you engage better, as it makes your goal more attainable.
3. *Add dates as deadlines for your overall goal as well as its steps.* Milton H. Erickson said, *'A goal without a date is just a dream.'* So true, isn't it? When you think of the goals you have in mind, the things you'd like to be, do and have, it can sometimes feel vague and fuzzy. Frame these by adding a completion date – both for your overall goal and its steps along the way. Adding dates helps you to engage better as it makes your goal more tangible.

This 3-step strategy helps you to engage your brain to its best as you take action. Your actions are moving you and your life, career, organization forward. Where you are today is the direct reflection of the thoughts, decisions, and actions you took days, months and years ago, which actually means that where you will be tomorrow will be a direct reflection of the thoughts, decisions, and actions you are about to take now.

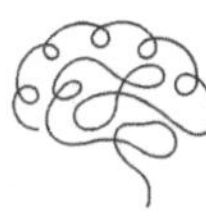

All the steps as part of this wire strategy belong to what we refer to as *cognitive control.* Also called *executive function*, cognitive control is the scientific name used to describe a series of neurocognitive processes – the functions – especially required for the control of behaviour to facilitate your goals.

These functions – think of them as thinking processes, such as planning, working memory, cognitive flexibility, strategizing, sequencing, problem-solving and set-shifting, to name a few – develop progressively in your brain over the years. Using neuroplasticity, these can be improved and strengthened as you learn and grow.

You know how much I believe in awareness, right? I particularly love teaching this topic in the workplace and see employees, who had mistakenly thought that such and such functions were out of their reach, discover that these can in fact be within their reach. By being a mindful leader, you can tune in your awareness to identify your weaknesses and your strengths to help you focus on your executive functions. From there, use the power of your mind to rewire your brain and intensify the strengths of your executive functions.

The name 'cognitive control' was first coined by Michael Posner, a psychologist and influencer in this field in 1975; however, the earliest mention of these functions is attributed to Donald Broadbent, also a psychologist, in the 1940s. Neuroscientists and neuropsychologists have continued their research to bring us the insights we've learned so far.

The PreFrontal Cortex (PFC), located in the frontal lobe of your brain, is the region of your brain that is primarily involved in cognitive control. Within your PFC, thanks to neuroimaging studies, scientists have been able to match specific regions with specific functions. So, for instance, the dorsolateral PreFrontal Cortex (dlPFC) is associated with the functions I've listed above – if you put your hand right at the top of your forehead and then shift it back by about an inch, you will know where your dlPFC is.

Now that we've learned a bit more about our cognitive control and its functions, let's tie in our 3-step wire strategy and the science.

1. *Plan.* Spending time on your plan engages your cognitive control from the get-go. As you plan, you strategize, you prioritize, you sequence. It increases efficiency while reducing risks. All these action steps to manage and achieve your goal are leveraging these executive functions: planning; strategizing; sequencing. In addition, when you face adversity and alter the plan of action, you are utilizing a few more functions: cognitive flexibility, problem-solving and set-shifting. These help you to adjust flexibly to the unexpected as well as reduce the uncertainty, thus avoiding triggering the threat response.
2. *Chunks.* Breaking your goal into chunks engages your cognitive control at several levels. We've already covered the reward system, and here it is also relevant, as instead of only assigning a reward for the overall goal completion, you get to assign a series of rewards for each of the chunks along the

way! This seriously builds momentum, and the dopamine releases help you stay motivated. Talking about dopamine, you'll also experience its good vibes effect as you tick off or strike through your various chunks.

3. *Dates.* Adding dates engages your cognitive control at a high level as, thanks to your PFC, you get to utilize the planning executive function. Plus, here let's add another layer. Studies have shown that when it comes to deadlines, we respond with a higher sense of urgency when it is phrased in a number of days, so in addition to your goal-completion date and step-completion dates, do also specify these in deadlines – in other words, avoid thinking of a quarter deadline for instance and instead think of it as a 90-day one.

Last but not least, I want to mention your working memory; studies have demonstrated that on average as adults we hold 3 to 5 chunks of information in our working memory, so breaking down your goal into chunks helps your productivity – you already knew this even if only unconsciously, as I'm sure you can relate to walking into a room and not remembering why you went there in the first place. This is because during your journey to that room, you thought of more than 3 to 5 items, and you forgot the original item you needed. Knowing this, you perform better when focusing on the next chunk and then the next one and then the next one.

And here you go: you now have this ENGAGE strategy that you can use whenever you need to. You can apply it for any of your goals as this *procrastination* challenge comes up for you. Next, the '3.2' wire strategy within this circuit…!

WIRE 3.2

IMPACTFUL CONFIDENCE – STRATEGY: EXPECT

This is where we are building the second of the 3 *Impactful Confidence* wires as part of your *Act with Impactful Confidence* circuit. As you can see from the highlighted part of this circuit framework in Illustration 15, this is the *Impactful Confidence – Expect* wire on your path.

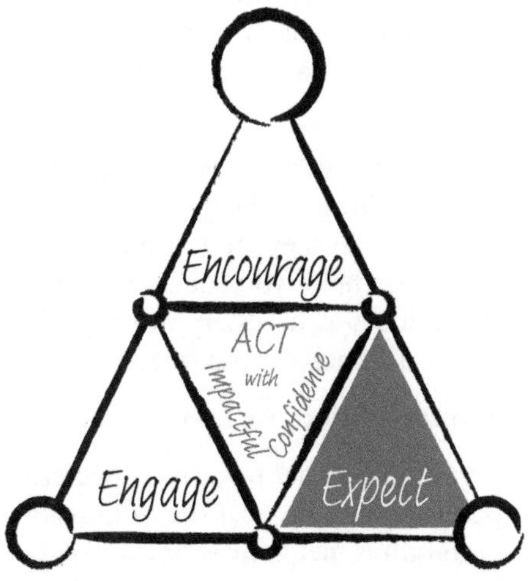

Illustration 15: The *Lead Beyond The Edge* Impactful Confidence – Expect Wire framework

One of the reasons why I'm so passionate about the power of awareness is that knowledge gives us the confidence to move forward. By tuning in your awareness – and we've been discovering ways to do that throughout this book already – you not only expand your understanding of yourself, but also thanks to this book's science teachings, you gain scientific insights into how your brain works. That way, you can make it work for you, and confidently take action.

Now that we have engaged the thinking component of our impactful confident state of mind, let's focus on the *feeling* component. This second strategy overcomes action inertia, which can occur by miscalculating what happens as a result of your actions. This makes you feel deflated, and it negatively impacts your next action.

So, when you find yourself disappointed by your progress towards your goal, tune in your awareness by...

Turning your focus to your expectations.

EXPECT is our second wire strategy.

Expectations are beliefs that things will unfold a certain way. They help us to make sense of our world. And, whether or not you had realized it before now, you expect things to turn out a certain way for absolutely everything you do. This is a behaviour of ours that we most often do not realize we do – most of our expectations are formulated at an unconscious level.

Remember how I said that with our inner dialogue we need to control it as opposed to it controlling us? Here, it is all about management. Manage your expectations so they are not managing you. See this as data research: this strategy helps you collect the data so you can alter and adjust your behaviours as necessary to set positive, realistic and successful expectations for each of your outcomes.

There are 3 layers to expectations we need to take into account:

1. Your expectation is either positive or negative.
2. Your expectation is either realistic or unrealistic.
3. Your expectation is met, unmet or exceeded.

Let's run through these together. The first layer is very straightforward; the second one is crucial, particularly focusing on avoiding setting unrealistic expectations. The more unrealistic an expectation is, the more risk it will not be met. Unrealistic expectations are also destructive and bound to fail; they set you off the wrong way.

As for the third layer: the first one happens when your outcome matches what you were expecting to happen. So this is when you take action towards your goal and you progress exactly as you had expected to. The second one is the opposite scenario, when your outcome does not match what you were expecting, and this brings you to a disappointing stall. And the third type is when your outcome not only matches what you were expecting to happen but surprises you with its even bigger impact and success.

Getting your expectations right, by accurately expecting what will happen throughout the goal achievement journey, is important as it keeps you motivated to keep going. The strategy is actionable: the only thing you need to do in order to uncover your expectations is to make the time to pause and ask yourself: '*What do I expect to happen?*' Think of your goal, and particularly focus on the next milestone along the way: that action and its outcome. Got it? Now answer that question with the how, the how long, the when, the where…

Not only will this strategy help you to manage and set better expectations of your actions – by highlighting to you the list of criteria that you've thought of, so you are clearer about the outcome and how it is supposed to unfold in alignment with your expectations – but you will also discover the reason why sometimes you simply are not driven to do something.

Indeed, what makes this strategy extra interesting is that by making the time to clarify your expectation about a particular outcome, you could discover that, unknown to you up to then, you are having a negative expectation about it. This prevents you from falling into the trap of feeling discouraged about your progress. When you consciously expect, you know what you are after and it helps you match your actions to meet it.

This is important as, even if unconsciously to you, your brain picks up on it and you feel out of sorts, hesitant and discouraged about your actions. It does make sense when you think about it: how can you be excited to drive towards an outcome for which you have set a negative expectation?

This impactful, yet simple question does what it needs to do by helping you bring something to the surface, uncovering something that you had not realized you were even thinking. I find this especially fascinating and I use it all the time, both for myself and with clients. There is such strength in having our expectations and our outcomes align: imagine using this at work with your team members and colleagues!

Science

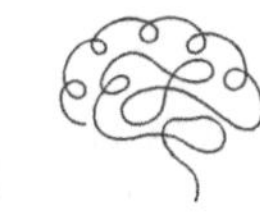

Let's add the science to back all this up, so you learn how to expect the best out of your brain as you take action by understanding what's going on in that head of yours when it comes to expectations.

We are going to learn some more neurochemistry, focusing on 2 neurochemicals at play. First, a familiar neurochemical player… Can you guess? Yes, you're right: dopamine! We've also spoken about the other one, the one nicknamed the stress hormone… yes, cortisol it is!

Both *dopamine* and *cortisol* are linked to your expectations. Let's look at what happens for each of the expectations layers and how these impact your brain chemistry – again here, I cannot emphasize it enough: this may be unconscious to you, but your brain does pick up on it:

1. *Negative/positive.* When you have a negative expectation about something, your brain senses a threat and releases cortisol; as a result, your anxiety level goes up. When you have a positive expectation about something, your brain senses a reward and releases dopamine; as a result, your motivation level goes up.
2. *Unrealistic/realistic.* Unrealistic expectations trigger cortisol; realistic expectations trigger dopamine. Same results as above.
3. *Unmet/met/exceeded.* When one of your expectations is unmet, you experience a dopamine fall: that is painful and you feel bad, frustrated and terribly disappointed; when it is met, you experience a dopamine release and yes, you know what that means – bring on the good vibes, the motivation, the anticipation, the drive; and when it is exceeded, you experience an even higher dopamine release, so fireworks all around.

As you manage your expectations, you learn how to manage the stress and the excitement surrounding your behaviours. As leaders, this is also particularly relevant at work. You have it in you to avoid negative, unrealistic and unsuccessful expectations. Plus, this also links to your performance; indeed, your PFC requires the right levels of dopamine in order for you to be able to focus. So, expect, expect and expect.

When activated, this wire strategy helps you manage your expectations better, adjusting these as necessary, as well as adjusting your plan of action towards an outcome on your goal achievement journey. By leveraging the power of expectations, you boost happiness, motivation and performance – yours and those of others. This is effective and impactful behaviour.

And here you go: you now have this EXPECT strategy that you can use whenever you need to. You can apply it for any of your goals as this *procrastination* challenge comes up for you. Next, the '3.3' wire strategy within this circuit…!

WIRE 3.3

IMPACTFUL CONFIDENCE – STRATEGY: ENCOURAGE

This is where we are building the third of the 3 *Impactful Confidence* wires as part of your *Act with Impactful Confidence* circuit. As you can see from the highlighted part of this circuit framework in Illustration 16, this is the *Impactful Confidence – Encourage* wire on your path.

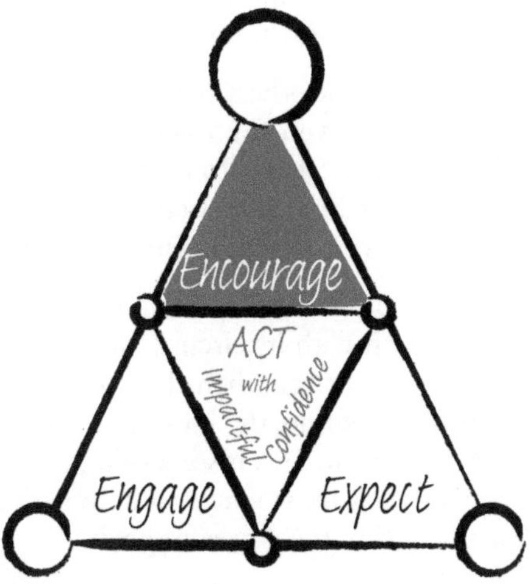

Illustration 16: The *Lead Beyond The Edge* Impactful Confidence – Encourage Wire framework

We're on the home stretch! This is our third strategy, having now covered the thinking and the feeling components of our confident state of mind, the one we want to step into on a daily basis. Here we are wrapping it up by covering the *acting* component. So that you lead

beyond the edge, thinking confidently, feeling confidently and now acting confidently.

Have you ever found yourself frazzled and a bit all over the place when taking action towards a goal and thought, *'I wish there was a way to be more organized in my approach!'* You know me by now, right? Of course, there is a way, and this is exactly the focus of our third wire strategy.

So, when you find yourself scattered about your goal…

ENCOURAGE your grey matter to be more consistent.

Encourage is our third wire strategy, and it fits perfectly here. One of the very first things I shared with you, right at the beginning of this book, is how amazing you and your brain are, and how you are able to use the power of your mind to rewire your brain using your brain-blowing neuroplasticity ability. And you've certainly been doing that, having formed 3 new circuits, including 11 new wires, so far!

This is the last wire and, like the others, it will stick, upon you repeating their consistent activation as you strengthen more and more each of these neural pathways. The best way to encourage your brain to take action in a better way – as in a more organized way: more focused, more efficient, more consistent – is to encourage habit formation.

Forming a habit works the same way as you've been forming your *Lead Beyond The Edge* path with its circuits and wires. The more you activate these, the more you strengthen the bold path in your brain. The more you perform an action, the more you strengthen its neural pathway, thus forming a habit. This is something you can confidently activate whenever you want to, as you would do with a snap of your fingers when you take action towards your goals.

You know, I did not always have a passion for the power of simplicity; over the years, I've thought and reflected about my past and my behaviours, as well as working with clients for over 2 decades, helping them lead to their extraordinary, and it is my belief that wanting and needing things to be complicated is a way to mask insecurities, especially those related to self-worth. With simplicity, you present yourself with no hiding, and there is strength in that.

This wire strategy is based on 2 simple, yet strong models, both discovered in the 1990s:

1. the Habit Loop
2. the 'If–Then' Plan.

Don't you love their names already? I get excited thinking of a loop – because the last powerful feedback loop we learned about gave us the knowledge to infinite motivation towards our goals, and then thinking about a plan – well, I do love a good plan, as I know it engages the executive functions and my brain loves me for it!

So we now know of 2 models to implement the Encourage wire strategy, and in our next *Science* accompanying section, I'm taking you through each of these in greater detail, so you can learn how to practically apply them to encourage your behaviours to become habits, thus saving you time and energy, and increasing your performance by saving brain power.

This circuit is all about behaviours. As such, I thought I'd share with you the 2 behaviour systems that scientists have uncovered. These were first thought to be competing with each other, but more recent studies have shown that they are in fact simultaneously competing and complementary:

- the goal-directed system
- the habit system.

We've learned about the *goal-directed system* already, and now you have its scientific name. The behaviours that fit within this system are the actions you take consciously and deliberately – these are regulated by your PFC. These goal-directed behaviours are cognitively heavy, infrequent and slow.

The behaviours that fit within the *habit system* are the actions you take less consciously and more automatically – these can be traced to your basal ganglia. These habitual behaviours are cognitively light, frequent and fast.

It is up to you to decide to shift a goal-directed behaviour from the goal-directed system onto the habit system, thus transforming it into a habitual behaviour, which is, of course, called a habit.

And, here are our 2 scientifically proven models to guide you when forming habits.

- *The Habit Loop*. This model was first discovered – using mice, a maze and chocolate – by a team of scientists at the Massachusetts Institute of Technology (MIT). Its simplicity is purely empowering and having learned about the various parts of the model over the last few sections, you are going to get it in a jiffy! The model comprises 3 parts, which are going to sound very familiar: Trigger –> Routine –> Reward.

The *trigger* is the cue that kick-starts the loop. It could be anything that encourages a behaviour – a prior action, a specific time, a feeling, a location, an event; make it predictable. The *routine* is the behaviour itself. The *reward* is... well, we know all about rewards, don't we? Make it creative, fun and satisfying; it needs to be so attractive that you do the behaviour to get it. And that's it, that's how this model works.

Let's do it, as in, let's set up one together now using this model. Think of your goal. Got it? Now think of its actions as chunks. List 3 to 5 and pick one behaviour you'd love to form as a habit; something that when you do it, day in, day out, will bring you closer to your goal completion. Got it? Now, think of the reward: what will your reward be when you reach your chunk outcome? Got it? This model of course follows what we've learned about the reward system, so your dopamine will be at play supporting you. And last but not least, think of the trigger: what will trigger you to do that specific behaviour? Got it? YAY, you are all set!

- *The 'If–Then' Plan.* As it is most commonly known, the if–then plan is called *implementation intention* in more scientific circles, and was introduced by psychologist Peter Gollwitzer in 1999. Remember when we learned about expectations and the strategic question to ask yourself, to which you would explicitly answer with the how, when and where? This question is going to be useful here too, as it will help you frame the desired behaviour to reach your specific outcome.

This proven model demonstrates how much more efficient it is to state a behaviour using the 'If–Then' Plan compared with a vaguer intention, which does not have a high rate of successful completion. So that it's always actionable and straightforward, simply fill in the blanks: IF [trigger] THEN I will [behaviour].

Let's do it, as in let's set up one together now using this model. Thanks to your practice with the previous model, you have your list of behaviours, so pick another specific one. Got it? Now, think of a new trigger. Got it? YAY, you are all set!

Both models help you strengthen the new habit pathway that you've built: make it grow strong by repeating, repeating and repeating some more. And the next thing you know, you will have a new habit on your hands – well, in your brain – ready to be activated effortlessly.

It is no coincidence that this wire is one of the *Impactful Confidence* ones: the higher your confidence, the easier your willpower will be to exercise. Commit, trust your brain plasticity and the Hebb's Rule findings, and fire up those neurons together: activate, activate, activate. This is how you become a confident self-directed learner and achiever. Follow either of these habit models, celebrate along the way to keep the dopamine flowing and successfully encourage habits through repetition.

And here you go: you now have this ENCOURAGE strategy that you can use whenever you need to. You can apply it for any of your goals as this *procrastination* challenge comes up for you. Next, not a surprise section anymore, as you know what's coming…!

Continuing to be as practical as possible for you, you'll find a working example, so that you can see how these strategies practically work to tackle a *procrastination* challenge thanks to its *Lead Beyond The Edge* solutions.

Let's fire it up!

Wire 3.1: Impactful Confidence – Strategy: Engage

Wire 3.2: Impactful Confidence – Strategy: Expect

Wire 3.3: Impactful Confidence – Strategy: Encourage

Scenario ▶ Merge, restructure and lead your new entire department.

You've just been informed that your team is merging with another team within your organization and you'll now be leading this new entire department. You are ready and excited – this is a great promotion. You want to do it BUT you are suddenly experiencing procrastination: you feel stuck, unsure and unable to take action.

The 3.1 solution
▶ Activate the ENGAGE wire strategy.

So much uncertainty about the how to proceed as you have so much to do: this is a big change and it is impacting you, your team, this new team, the entire department and the whole organization. You realize you need to ENGAGE your cognitive functions, so you start putting in place a plan of action: you get clear on your overall goal and chunk it down into manageable steps. Adding dates makes your overall goal and its milestones more tangible. You start focusing on that one next step and move forward.

The 3.2 solution
▶ Activate the EXPECT wire strategy.

This promotion was unexpected, and you know that it is time to clarify what's ahead for you and this now larger department, and EXPECT. You ask yourself: *'What is expected from me with this new role?' 'What do I expect to achieve in the next 90 days?'* The answers are helping you manage your expectations and draw out plans accordingly now that you consciously know the how long, the when, the where... Your expectations are positive and realistic, and you feel confident about meeting and even exceeding them. Having set clear expectations, you and your teams are aligned with your actions, driven and motivated to make it happen.

The 3.3 solution
▶ Activate the ENCOURAGE wire strategy.

There is a lot to do: from communicating the changes due to the merger to helping your existing and new team members navigate through the reorganization, so that they can grow from it, and so much more. You sit down and look at your plan of action and start seeing some actions that, should they become consistent, will support you on your way forward.

You ENCOURAGE this habit formation by either using the Habit Loop model, where you identify the trigger, the routine and the reward or the 'If–Then' Plan model, where you fill in the blanks: IF [trigger] THEN I will [behaviour]. You feel organized and focused: this new habit helps you be more efficient and consistent, and you perform better.

Any and all of these strategies are helping you move forward with impactful confidence as you take charge and push through your comfort zone. You are doing it: you are leading beyond the edge, embracing your promotion and leading your new entire department.

You DO it!

And *voilà*, there you have them: my 3 actionable strategies to help you stop procrastination. If your actions are lacking, **engage, expect** and **encourage** your way to impactful confidence to reach your 'I DO it!' success point. Each of these represents one of the *Impactful Confidence* wires as part of our third circuit, which you've now entirely built!!!

You will find a recap text version of what you've accomplished in the next section. As for now, I know you are expecting me to close a certain story I opened at the beginning of this *Impactful Confidence* circuit, right? So, where were we? *Here I was, surrounded by books, overwhelmed by the magnitude of the project and stuck…*

Story

'Getting assigned to a special project and tackling it!'

After a few minutes, I confidently stood up and looked at the mountains of books: it was a mess in here, but I began to see how to start making it happen. I closed my eyes and imagined what was expected at the finish line:

I could see the enhanced library, all organized, aligned and arranged, and I could see a big proud smile on Grand-Père's face.

This was big, but it was exciting too. I thought to myself: 'Okay, I'm doing it.' And I knew how and where to start my plan of action: one book at a time. I felt engaged, revved up to go, and committed to making it happen. After pushing most of the piles towards the walls, I was now standing in front of one single pile of books I could focus on.

And off I went: one book after another book after another book. Over the next few days, I encouraged the repetition of the task at hand: one pile after another after another. Next thing I knew, I had completed my mission. Standing by the door of the library, I called Grand-Père, grinning from ear to ear and theatrically opened the door as I said to him, 'Ta-da…!' I sure was proud as punch!!!

RECAP CIRCUIT 3/3

ACT with IMPACTFUL CONFIDENCE

Triple WooHoo!

You have now built your third and last circuit and its 4 wires!!! So let's have fun with the celebration you've been expecting: how are you going to top your last reward? Do it! Celebrate your amazing progress along the path and get excited as you are so much closer to extraordinary results: there is no stopping you now!

You have used the power of your mind to rewire your brain to create your third circuit and its 4 wires as part of your *Lead Beyond The Edge* bold path. Now continue to strengthen it with repetition every time you activate it. With neuroplasticity, the more you do it, the less you'll have to do it!

Here is a recap text version of what you've accomplished.

Let's Fire It ALL Up!

Lead Beyond The Edge, Circuit 3/3

Activate your third circuit
to help you strengthen your behaviours,
stop procrastination and move from…

Can I do it?

ACT with Impactful Confidence

- Overarching Wire 3: Act
    - Intro Wires: Impactful Confidence
        - Wire 3.1: Impactful Confidence – Strategy: Engage
        - Wire 3.2: Impactful Confidence – Strategy: Expect
        - Wire 3.3: Impactful Confidence – Strategy: Encourage
- Recap Circuit 3/3: Act with Impactful Confidence

… to

I DO it!

Multisensory Learning Boosts: Circuit 3/3

This is the third recap section, so you know what's coming: the home stretch!!! It is time to leverage the power of our olfactory, tactile and auditory senses by applying these 3 science-backed strategies again.

Here are your instructions for you to implement the *multisensory learning boosts* for your third newly built circuit and its wires – again here, the cues, the kinaesthetic anchor and the visualization are different as these now apply to this third circuit.

Let's continue engaging and boosting your learning using your olfactory sense:

- Pick the same scent you've picked before. This is important, as you are scent training your brain: the same scent will help you cue it again so that you continue strengthening the pathways.
- Smell it (inhale or diffuse) and reflect on this particular circuit and its wires, and their teachings (which have now been stored as memories in your brain) and write down 3 to 5 insights you've gained as you've built your third circuit. Think of the 4 strategies: Act + Engage, Expect, Encourage; alternate scent and writing – this will lead you to associate the scent you've chosen with your learning.
- Then sleep.
- Enjoy and repeat!

Let's continue engaging and boosting your learning using your tactile sense:

Here your state is *Act with Impactful Confidence* and your stimulus is the third kinaesthetic anchor I've created for you.

- Elicit the desired state. I'm going to give you 2 steps – remember, the stronger your state, the stronger the anchor.
- *First step:* Read out loud the 3 to 5 insights you've compiled as part of our first learning boost. Make sure these start with 'I…' to fully engage with them; this is about eliciting your state, so go beyond reading and perform these to really feel your insights' impact.
- As you do that, it is time to set your third kinaesthetic anchor, the one for this third circuit and its wires. To form it, choose the same hand you've picked for the first and second anchors, then snap your fingers (build tension between your middle finger and your thumb and then move your middle finger forcefully down alongside your thumb towards your palm) a couple of times while reading your notes.
- *Second step:* Recall a time when you had that 'do it' behaviour, when it felt like: 'Yes, I DO it!' and then you moved forward to achieve your goal – got it? Step into the memory and be as descriptive as possible: What does it feel like? What do you see? Hear? Touch? Maybe even smell and taste? Feel it throughout your body.
- As you do that, repeat your anchor: snap your fingers a couple of times while reliving your memory.
- Release your anchor when you feel at your best, when the peak of the intensity is reached.
- (Optional) Play in the background another one of your favourite energizing songs as you create your anchor.
- Test it. To do so, remember you first have to break your state, which I can help you do by asking you a question that's going to get you to think of something else: so tell me, what is your mother's maiden name? Now that the state has been broken, it is time to fire your anchor. Two things can happen: you will either recall that state or just not yet; most anchors need a couple of times to be fully formed, so simply repeat the process.
- Enjoy and repeat!

Let's continue engaging and boosting your learning using your auditory sense:

- Set aside 15 minutes.
- Seat yourself in a comfortable and undisturbed place.
- Have your computer or your phone with you on do-not-disturb, so you can access the third visualization, but make sure you have turned off emails and any social media alerts so that you maximize your experience.
- Listen to it. You don't need to do anything else, as I will guide you to reflect on this third circuit and its wires helping you think back over your learning and reinforce insights you've gained.
- (Optional) If you are like me and some of my clients, you will want to write down some of the thoughts that popped up during this experience, so you will need this next step. Capture what came up – thoughts, decisions, actions – to continue leading you on your goal journey.
- Enjoy and repeat!

Continue using these stimuli so you can trigger yet another set of *Lead Beyond The Edge* memories, this time a particular series of insights you gained as you read and built your third circuit and its wires, whenever you decide to do so.

Thanks to all of these *multisensory learning boosts*, you now have at your fingertips (literally and physically) any part of your *Lead Beyond The Edge* path and can recall powerful memories and supportive states to support you along the way as you achieve your goals. This is exactly what I meant when I first said in the *Launch Circuit* that this is not *just* a book.

And this wraps up your third circuit, with its **ACT** overarching wire and its 3 *Impactful Confidence* wires, **ENGAGE**, **EXPECT** and **ENCOURAGE**, as part of your *Lead Beyond The Edge* bold path. Next, you are going to access your *Recap Circuit* to further enhance your journey as you make the extraordinary happen.

As for now, I know you are expecting me to close a certain story I opened at the beginning of this ACT circuit, right? So, where were we? *Here I was, months and months after I had said I would do something and yet with nothing to show for it, wondering if I should backpedal or push through…*

Story

'Dreaming of writing a book and becoming a published author!'

'WOW: stop right there, Frederique!' These questions, doubts and insecurities surprised me a lot; it was as if I needed to hear myself think those thoughts to then act and blast them away. No way this was even a possibility. Nope. Non. No. I knew what was going on. I was overwhelmed. I was confused. And I was scared.

Okay, yes, I had fallen off track, but I reminded myself of what I tell my clients: 'You've fallen off track? That's okay and there is good news: this means that there is a track for you to get back on, and that's amazing.' Plus, I found myself adding another perspective: that fear actually meant I was right on track about to break through a new level. How exciting was this!

That fear was a reflection of how big I was playing. Definitely not playing safe. It was time to make it happen – my castle in the air; time for the foundations. Time to leave the comfort of my zone, push the wall, and stretch and grow. I knew it at the core of my being: it was time to lead beyond the edge.

So I did, and took that next step, by simply focusing on that next step and the reward it would get me. This felt incredible. My brain was on board and all I needed to do was to simply signal to it. Such a 'good vibes' hit: I felt motivated and I could not wait until I'd take the next action, and then the next one, and then the next one, and then the next one. I was doing it.

I felt grounded. I smiled: I know it is a great place for me to be. When I'm grounded on and off stage, I'm in flow and I deliver to the best of my ability serving my audience. So, yes this was right. And more than 50,000 words later, which I wrote in 12 weeks while confined during the pandemic, here we are: as you read this, you are holding my book in your hands.

That moment is everything I could ever imagine, and as the anticipation of what's yet to come continues to fuel me, I proudly struck through my 'Write a book' item off my legacy goal list. I DID IT!!!

RECAP
CIRCUIT

On our journey together we've progressed
through a series of specific steps on our bold path:
the one you have consciously followed since page 1,
as you were building each of its circuits and wires,
leveraging the power of your mind to rewire your brain.

You did it!
You have now built your entire *Lead Beyond The Edge* path.
How exciting is that!

I'm absolutely thrilled for you.

There is nothing I love to do more in my work than seeing you achieve your extraordinary results by leading beyond the edge. Simply activate the path or any of the circuits or wires of your choice, and SNAP, make it happen.

As I was writing this book, I was thinking of you (I'm sure you've noticed – it sure has been a pleasure connecting with you throughout the book!) and I wanted to include a special section, which I decided to call *Recap Circuit* in order to provide you with a few extra content inserts to further enhance your journey towards your extraordinary results.

So, let's do it!

THE FULL PATH FRAMEWORK

This is the full *Lead Beyond The Edge* framework – you have not seen it in its entirety since the very beginning of this book, so I thought it would be useful to put it here for you.

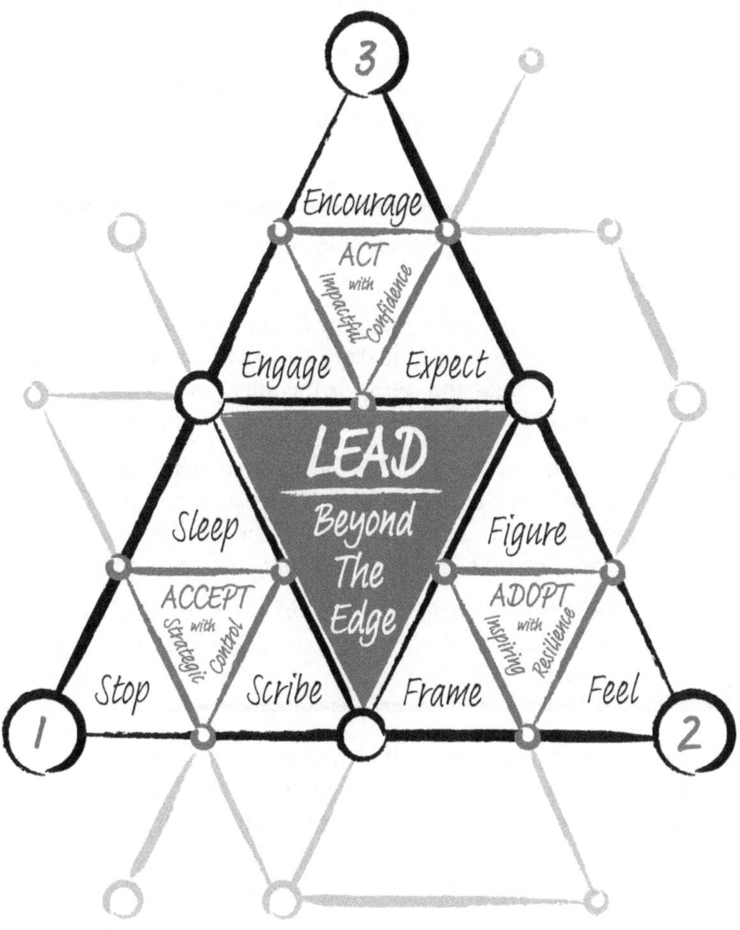

Illustration 17: The *Lead Beyond The Edge* full framework

You will find information about how to access a printable version of this framework within the *Resources* section of this *Recap Circuit*. That way, you can download, print and place it in your office, both at work and at home.

On our journey together, we've progressed through a series of specific steps on our bold path – the one you have consciously followed since page 1, as you were building each of its circuits and wires, leveraging the power of your mind to rewire your brain.

This 1 bold path is a network of 3 circuits and 12 wires. By now, you are very familiar with it: you have seen it throughout the entire book as we were progressing along the path leading you to extraordinary results.

Going forward, there are a couple of ways you can use this framework:

- *To strengthen your newly built neural pathways.* Place it where you can see it daily, so it will act as a learning visual trigger and jolt your memory; every time you see it, launch your kinaesthetic anchors and fire it up.
- *To pinpoint where you are on your goal journey as you face a particular challenge.* Identify the relevant circuit and decide to either activate it as a whole or pick one of its wires so you can overcome it and continue doing it.
- *To highlight a specific circuit or wire on which you particularly want to work.* Use a highlighter marker and circle or trace the area of your focus.

I know that the framework itself already acts as a powerful executive visual summary, and just in case you would benefit from a text-based one too, I've prepared one for you next. You will also find information about how to access a printable version of this text-based framework within this *Recap Circuit* in the *Resources* section.

You now have your bold path to extraordinary results wired into your brain, and the only question left to answer is *'What's your next "I want to do it" goal?'* And then SNAP, lead beyond the edge, and next thing you know you will be at the 'I DID IT!!!' stage again.

Your Lead Beyond The Edge Path!

Start

I want to do it.

Activate your first circuit
to help you strengthen your beliefs,
control your inner dialogue and move from…

Can I?

ACCEPT with Strategic Control
CIRCUIT 1/3

- Overarching Wire 1: Accept
    - Intro Wires: Strategic Control
        - Wire 1.1: Strategic Control – Strategy: Stop
        - Wire 1.2: Strategic Control – Strategy: Scribe
        - Wire 1.3: Strategic Control – Strategy: Sleep
- Recap Circuit 1/3: Accept with Strategic Control

… to

I CAN!

Activate your second circuit to help you strengthen your attitudes, overcome adversity and move from…

Do I have it?

ADOPT with Inspiring Resilience CIRCUIT 2/3

- Overarching Wire 2: Adopt
  - Intro Wires: Inspiring Resilience
    - Wire 2.1: Inspiring Resilience – Strategy: Frame
    - Wire 2.2: Inspiring Resilience – Strategy: Feel
    - Wire 2.3: Inspiring Resilience – Strategy: Figure
- Recap Circuit 2/3: Adopt with Inspiring Resilience

… to

I CAN-DO it!

Activate your third circuit
to help you strengthen your behaviours,
stop procrastination and move from…

Can I do it?

ACT with Impactful Confidence
CIRCUIT 3/3

- Overarching Wire 3: Act
  - Intro Wires: Impactful Confidence
    - Wire 3.1: Impactful Confidence – Strategy: Engage
    - Wire 3.2: Impactful Confidence – Strategy: Expect
    - Wire 3.3: Impactful Confidence – Strategy: Encourage
- Recap Circuit 3/3: Act with Impactful Confidence

… to

I DO it!

End (or is the end only the beginning?!)

SNAP

I DID IT!!!

THE MANIFESTO

This is your *Lead Beyond The Edge* manifesto!

You will find information about how to access a printable version of the manifesto in the *Resources* section. That way, you can download, print and place it in your office, both at work and at home. Place it where you can see it daily, so it will act as a learning visual trigger and jolt your memory; every time you see it, launch your kinaesthetic anchors and fire it up.

The Lead Beyond The Edge Manifesto!

When I lead beyond the edge, I accept, adopt and act through my fears, thus achieving my goals in an approach that is both results-driven and mindful. This bold path guides me to successfully go from the exciting 'I want to do it' stage to the exhilarating 'I DID IT!!!' stage on my trailblazing goal journey.

Everything I want to achieve starts in my brain, ignited and fuelled by my beliefs, supported and influenced by my attitudes and brought to fruition by my aligned behaviours. My awareness leads to change.

With the belief that I CAN, that unshakeable belief that I really truly believe, the CAN-DO attitude that keeps me going no matter what and the DO IT behaviour that continually and consistently drives and sustains momentum, I MAKE IT HAPPEN.

I use the power of my mind to rewire my brain for success, so that I control my inner dialogue, I overcome adversity and I stop procrastination. I simply take charge of my mind to get the results that I want, and I actively leverage neuroplasticity, this remarkable ability of mine, to repeatedly direct my brain to go up the path I lead it to.

When I lead beyond the edge, I step up and I lead myself, my team, my organization. Nothing stops me in my tracks: I am not letting my thoughts stop me, I am not letting anything that happens stop me and I am not letting my confidence stop me.

I am unstoppable.

I push through:

- If my thoughts get in the way, I stop, scribe and sleep my way to strategic control to reach my 'I CAN!' success point.
- If things happen around me, I frame, feel and figure my way to inspiring resilience to reach my 'I CAN-DO it!' success point.
- If my actions are lacking, I engage, expect and encourage my way to impactful confidence to reach my 'I DO it!' success point.

I consciously and mindfully take responsibility for my beliefs, my attitudes and my behaviours and I commit to my goals. I trust and follow the framework that spans all of the goal journey. I have built my success path with its circuits and wires and can now activate them whenever I need to, strengthening their pathways, remain in the 'I'm doing it' flow and reach my goals: anything, anytime, anywhere.

It is time.

SNAP: I lead beyond the edge and achieve my extraordinary results!!!

RESOURCES

I'd love to continue supporting you on your journey to extraordinary results. To that end, I've created a dedicated accompanying membership website for this book, where you can view and download further resources, such as the *Lead Beyond The Edge*:

- full framework (visual and text-based)
- goal pledge
- music playlist
- audio visualizations
- kinaesthetic anchors
- videos
- checklists
- templates

and more!

Visit www.LeadBeyondTheEdge.com/member to access your complimentary resources now!

And, let's connect too.

I LOVE to connect and would love to hear your #LeadBeyondTheEdge success stories.

OFF STAGE, please reach out on any of the following social media channels:

LinkedIn: Frederique Murphy

Instagram: FrederiqueMurphy

Facebook: FrederiqueMurphyM3

Twitter: @IrishSmiley

Pinterest: IrishSmiley

YouTube: FrederiqueMurphy

ON STAGE, what a pleasure it would be to meet at an event too; for more details on how I can help you inspire and equip your teams and audiences to lead beyond the edge, contact my Speaking team, to discuss hiring me to keynote at your next event at speak@frederiquemurphy.com.

I'd love to help you and your organization step up even more, move forward and reach a new altitude, strengthening that path to extraordinary results.

I am looking forward to connecting with you, off and on stage.

As for now, there is only one thing left to do…

EPILOGUE

Story

'Leaving everything behind, and starting afresh!'

Because, we have arrived. I had landed. And as the flight attendant gave her welcoming announcement in both Irish Gaeilge and English, I chuckled and shook my head from side to side: I had no idea what she was saying and I'm not only talking about the Irish. 'Céad míle fáilte go Baile Átha Cliath! A warm welcome to Dublin!' *The only word I understood from the English version was Dublin. At least I was on Irish soil and I was smiling.*

I was here in Ireland. I had left the country where I was born, leaving everything behind except for my suitcase: one bag weighing 23 kilograms (50 pounds). I spoke no English, apart from 'hello' and 'thank you', yet I felt as if this was all meant to be. I was excited for whatever was going to happen, believing I would make it work. And scared too…

As I was waiting for my turn to disembark, I clearly remember taking the time to pause and ground myself. I was in a new country, where I knew no one and tomorrow I was starting my summer job: no wonder I was scared. I realized this was entirely normal.

With a pinch of pride, I reminded myself that I had gotten that job and this was going to work: I imagined walking in the European headquarters – I had prepped what I was going to say to the receptionist, hoping she would understand me and guide me directly to my French-speaking contact. I knew I could do it.

At this moment, I might not have known exactly what was in my future, but I did know exactly what to do next. It was time to disembark. Taking that next step. Literally, as one of the passengers had stopped to let me exit my row. Doing it felt good.

In hindsight, this was when the Lead Beyond The Edge path started to fire up and form in my brain. This was the intense instant that ignited it all. I can see myself going through each of the defining moments: the 'I CAN!'

belief and its acceptance, the 'I CAN-DO it!' attitude and its adoption, and the 'I DO it!' behaviour and its action.

Approaching the exit, I felt the cool breeze brush across my face, I snapped my fingers and smiled at the crew. 'Go raibh maith agat. Thank you.' *As I was walking down the plane stairs, I walked into the rest of my life. I was at the beginning of my journey: ready, committed and driven to make it happen. That moment was priceless. It led me on the bold path to extraordinary results.*

CONCLUSION

WOW, this is it…! Conclusion time, and at this stage I want to share a few more words with you and start by saying thank you. Thank YOU for trusting me to be your guide on this trailblazing journey, transforming beliefs, attitudes and behaviours to create lasting change in your life, at work and at home. From the bottom of my heart, it has been a pleasure to be by your side as you boldly built your *Lead Beyond The Edge* path to your extraordinary results.

As I shared with you at the beginning of this book, I believe that this framework was first ignited in my brain when I was 18 onboard a flight I will never ever forget. Since then, I've studied, worked and learned A LOT. Everything to bring me to this moment, when it was time to share it with you, enabling you to benefit from my experience and expertise and bypass 20 years by simply reading this book and applying its teachings.

This framework is one of my most prized creations and every time I get the opportunity to help someone achieve their extraordinary, whether on stage in front of an audience or here in front of you, my heart – which at one point in time felt broken – soars. And, so does my brain! Throughout this book, as I do from stage with my clients, I've shown you both my heart and my brain, and given you my all. I've purposely used personal stories to connect with you at a deep level to intensify your experience and your learning.

I appreciate the investment you've made in yourself, and I cannot wait to hear the #LeadBeyondTheEdge stories you are going to experience (if not already!) in your life, career and organization.

Be limitless with what you can achieve: the limits of your possibilities match the limits of your thinking. And always remember that when you lead beyond the edge, the extraordinary happens.

For now, this is goodbye, although I have a feeling that *ce n'est qu'un au revoir.*

Let's SNAP, SNAP, SNAP!!!

To your extraordinary results,
Frederique

Frederique Murphy

REFERENCES

Books

Launch Circuit

Hebb, D.O. (1949). *The organization of behavior: A neuropsychological theory*. Wiley.

Merzenich, M. (2013). *Soft-wired: How the new science of brain plasticity can change your life.* Parnassus.

Norman, D. (2007). The brain that changes itself: Stories of personal triumph from the frontiers of brain science. Viking Press.

Strode, M. (1903). *Wind-wafted wild flowers.* Open Court.

ACCEPT with Strategic Control Circuit

Grinder, J. and Bandler, R. (1989). *The structure of magic I: A book about language and therapy.* Science and Behavior Books.

Hannaford, C. (1995). *Smart moves: Why learning is not all in your head.* Great River Books.

Zinsser, N., Bunker, L. and Williams, J.M. (2010). 'Cognitive techniques for building confidence and enhancing performance'. In J.M. Williams (ed.), *Applied sport psychology: Personal growth to peak performance*. McGraw-Hill.

ADOPT with Inspiring Resilience Circuit

Allport, G. (1935). 'Attitudes', in *A Handbook of Social Psychology*, ed. C. Murchison. Clark University Press.

Csikszentmihalyi, M. (1990). Flow: *The psychology of optimal experience.* Harper and Row.

Damasio, A. (1994). *Descartes' error: Emotion, reason, and the human brain.* Putnam.

Darwin, C. (1872). *The expression of the emotions in man and animals*. J. Murray.

Goleman, D. (1995). *Emotional intelligence: Why it can matter more than IQ*. Bantam.

James, W. (1890). *The principles of psychology.* Henry Holt and Co.

Maltz, M. (1960). *Psycho-cybernetics*. Simon & Schuster.

Seligman, M. (1998). *Learned optimism: How to change your mind and your life.* Knopf.

ACT with Impactful Confidence Circuit

Cuddy, A. (2015). *Presence: Bringing your boldest self to your biggest challenges.* Little, Brown Spark.

Duhigg, C. (2012). *The power of habit: Why we do what we do in life and business.* Random House.

Durant, W. (1926). *The story of philosophy*. Simon & Schuster.

Kahneman, D. (2011). *Thinking, fast and slow.* Macmillan.

Parks-Stamm, E. and Gollwitzer, P. (2009). 'Goal implementation: The benefits and costs of IF–THEN planning.' In G.B. Moskowitz and H. Grant (eds), *The psychology of goals.* Guilford Press.

Scientific Papers

Introduction

Suzuki, W., Feliú-Mójer, M., Hasson, U., Yehuda, R. and Zarate, J.M. (2018). 'Dialogues: The science and power of storytelling.' *The Journal of Neuroscience*, 38(44), 9468–9470.

Launch Circuit

Bennett, E.L., Diamond, M.C., Drech, D. and Rosenzweig, M.R. (1964). 'Chemical and anatomical plasticity of brain.' *Science*, 146(3644), 610–619.

Drachman, D.A. (2005). 'Do we have brain to spare?' *Neurology*, 64(12), 2056–2062.

Han, J.H., Lee, H.J., Kang, H., Oh, S.H. and Lee, D.S. (2019). 'Brain plasticity can predict the Cochlear Implant outcome in adult-onset deafness.' *Frontiers in Human Neuroscience*, 13(38).

Herculano-Houzel, S. (2009). 'The human brain in numbers: A linearly scaled-up primate brain.' *Frontiers in Human Neuroscience*, 3(31).

Paraskevopoulos, E. and Herholz, S. (2013). 'Multisensory integration and neuroplasticity in the human cerebral cortex.' *Translational Neuroscience*, 4(3), 337–348.

Sasmita, A.O., Kuruvilla, J. and Pick Kiong Ling, A. (2018). 'Harnessing neuroplasticity: Modern approaches and clinical future.' *International Journal of Neuroscience*, 128(11), 1061–1077.

Shams, L. and Seitz, A.R. (2008). 'Benefits of multisensory learning.' *Trends in Cognitive Sciences*, 12(11), 411–417.

ACCEPT with Strategic Control Circuit

Arshamian, A., Iannilli, E., Gerber, J.C. et al. (2013). 'The functional neuroanatomy of odor evoked autobiographical memories cued by odors and words.' *Neuropsychologi*a, 51(1), 123–131.

Ben, Simon, E., Rossi, A., Harvey, A.G. and Walker, M.P. (2020). 'Overanxious and underslept.' *Nature Human Behaviour*, 4, 100–110.

Hart, S. and Hart, T. (2010). 'The future of cognitive behavioral interventions within behavioral medicine.' *Journal of Cognitive Psychotherapy*, 24(4), 344–353.

Hölzel, B.K., Carmody, J., Vangel, M., Congleton, C., Yerramsetti, S.M., Gard, T. and Lazar, S.W. (2011). 'Mindfulness practice leads to increases in regional brain gray matter density.' *Psychiatry Research*, 191(1), 36–43.

Kini, P., Wong, J., McInnis, S., Gabana, N. and Brown, J.W. (2016). 'The effects of gratitude expression on neural activity.' *Neuroimage*, 128, 1–10.

Lahl, O., Wispel, C., Willigens, B. and Pietrowsky, R. (2008). 'An ultra short episode of sleep is sufficient to promote declarative memory performance.' *Journal of Sleep Research*, 17(1), 3–10.

Lieberman, M.D., Eisenberger, N.I., Crockett, M.J., Tom, S.M., Pfeifer, J.H. and Way, B.M. (2007). 'Putting feelings into words: Affect labeling disrupts amygdala activity in response to affective stimuli.' *Psychological Science*, 18(5), 421–428.

Mednick, S., Nakayama, K. and Stickgold, R. (2003). 'Sleep-dependent learning: A nap is as good as a night.' *Nature Neuroscience*, 6(7), 697–698.

Milner, C. and Cote, K. (2009). 'Benefits of napping in healthy adults: Impact of nap length, time of day, age, and experience with napping.' *Journal of Sleep Research*, 18(2), 272–281.

Moss, M., Cook, J., Wesnes, K. and Duckett, P. (2003). 'Aromas of rosemary and lavender essential oils differentially affect cognition and mood in healthy adults.' *International Journal of Neuroscience*, 113(1), 15–38.

Neumann, F., Oberhauser, V. and Kornmeier, J. (2020). 'How odor cues help to optimize learning during sleep in a real life-setting.' *Scientific Reports*, 10(1), 1227.

Nishida, M. and Walker, M. (2007). 'Daytime naps, motor memory consolidation and regionally specific sleep spindles.' *PLoS ONE*, 2(4), e341.

Olofsson, J., Ekström, I., Sjölund, S., Lindström, J., Syrjänen, E., Neely, A., Nyberg, L. and Larsson, M. (2019). 'Smell-based memory training: Evidence of olfactory learning and transfer to a visual task.' *Chemical Senses*, 45(7), 593–600.

Pennebaker, J.W. (1993). 'Putting stress into words: Health, linguistic, and therapeutic implications.' *Behaviour Research and Therapy*, 31(6), 539–548.

Pennington, E. (2011). 'Brain-based learning theory: The incorporation of movement to increase the learning of grammar by high school students.' Doctoral dissertation, Liberty University.

Schacter, D.L., Addis, D.R., Hassabis, D., Martin, V.C., Spreng, R.N. and Szpunar, K.K. (2012). 'The future of memory: Remembering, imagining, and the brain.' *Neuron*, 76(4), 677–694.

Singleton, O., Hölzel, B.K., Vangel, M., Brach, N., Carmody, J. and Lazar, S.W. (2014). 'Change in brainstem gray matter concentration following a mindfulness-based intervention is correlated with improvement in psychological well-being.' *Frontiers in Human Neuroscience*, 8, 33.

Vyazovskiy, V.V. (2015). 'Sleep, recovery, and metaregulation: Explaining the benefits of sleep.' *Nature and Science of Sleep*, 7, 171–184.

Wood, A.M., Joseph, S., Lloyd, J. and Atkins, S. (2009). 'Gratitude influences sleep through the mechanism of pre-sleep cognitions.' *Journal of Psychosomatic Research*, 66(1), 43–48.

ADOPT with Inspiring Resilience Circuit

Buhle, T.J., Silvers, J.A., Wager, T.D., Lopez, R., Onyemekwu, C., Kober, H., Weber, J. and Ochsner, K.N. (2014). 'Cognitive reappraisal of emotion: A meta-analysis of human neuroimaging studies.' *Cerebral Cortex*, 24(11), 2981–2990.

Damasio, A. and Carvalho, G. (2013). 'The nature of feelings: Evolutionary and neurobiological origins.' *Nature Reviews Neuroscience*, 14(2), 143–152.

Donaldson, S., Dollwet, M. and Warren, M. (2014). 'Happiness, excellence, and optimal human functioning revisited: Examining the peer-reviewed literature linked to positive psychology.' *The Journal of Positive Psychology*, 10(3), 185–95.

Gross, J.J. (2002). 'Emotion regulation: Affective, cognitive, and social consequences.' *Psychophysiology*, 39(3), 281–91.

Harzer, C. and Ruch, W. (2012). 'The application of signature character strengths and positive experiences at work.' *Journal of Happiness Studies*, 14, 965–983.

LeDoux, J. (2012). 'Rethinking the emotional brain.' *Neuron*, 73(4), 653–676.

McRae, K., Hughes, B., Chopra, S., Gabrieli, J.D., Gross, J.J. and Ochsner, K.N. (2010). 'The neural bases of distraction and reappraisal.' *Journal of Cognitive Neuroscience*, 22(2), 248–262.

Melnychuk, M.C., Dockree, P.M., O'Connell, R.G., Murphy, P.R., Balsters, J.H. and Robertson, I.H. (2018). 'Coupling of respiration and attention via the locus coeruleus: Effects of meditation and pranayama.' *Psychophysiology*, 55(3), e13091.

Pascual-Leone, A., Nguyet, D., Cohen, L.G., Brasil-Neto, J.P., Cammarota, A. and Hallett, M. (1995). 'Modulation of muscle responses evoked by transcranial magnetic stimulation during the acquisition of new fine motor skills'. *Journal of Neurophysiology*, 74(3), 1037–1045.

Seligman, M. and Csikszentmihalyi, M. (2000). 'Positive psychology. An introduction.' *The American Psychologist*, 55(1), 5–14.

Wu, G., Feder, A., Cohen, H., Kim, J., Calderon, S., Charney, D. and Mathé, A. (2013). 'Understanding resilience.' *Frontiers in Behavioral Neuroscience*, 7(10), 10.

Youssef-Morgan, C. and Luthans, F. (2007). 'Positive organizational behavior in the workplace: The impact of hope, optimism, and resilience.' *Journal of Management*, 33(5), 774–800.

Zaccaro, A., Piarulli, A., Laurino, M., Garbella, E., Menicucci, D., Neri, B. and Gemignani, A. (2018). 'How breath-control can change your life: A systematic review on psycho-physiological correlates of slow breathing.' *Frontiers in Human Neuroscience*, 12, 353.

ACT with Impactful Confidence Circuit

Buschman, T.J. and Miller, E.K. (2014). 'Goal-direction and top-down control.' *Philosophical Transactions of the Royal Society of London. Series B, Biological Sciences*, 369(1655), 20130471.

Cortese, A., Amano, K., Koizumi, A. et al. (2016). 'Multivoxel neurofeedback selectively modulates confidence without changing perceptual performance.' *Nature Communications*, 7, 13669.

Covey, D. and Cheer, J. (2019). 'Accumbal dopamine release tracks the expectation of dopamine neuron-mediated reinforcement.' *Cell Reports,* 27(2), 481–490.

Cowan, N. (2010). 'The magical mystery four: How is working memory capacity limited, and why?' *Current Directions in Psychological Science*, 19(1), 51–57.

Cuddy, A.J.C., Schultz, S.J. and Fosse, N.E. (2018). 'P-curving a more comprehensive body of research on postural feedback reveals clear evidential value for power-posing effects: Reply to Simmons and Simonsohn.' *Psychological Science*, 29(4), 656-666.

Diamond, A. (2013). 'Executive functions.' *Annual Review of Psychology*, 64, 135–168.

Dolan, R.J. and Dayan, P. (2013). 'Goals and habits in the brain.' *Neuron*, 80(2), 312–325.

Ferreri, L., Mas-Herrero, E., Zatorre, R.J. et al. (2019). 'Dopamine modulates the reward experiences elicited by music.' *Proceedings of the National Academy of Science USA*, 116(9), 3793–3798.

Fonollosa, J., Neftci, E. and Rabinovich, M. (2015). 'Learning of chunking sequences in cognition and behavior.' *PLoS Computational Biology*, 11(11).

Gollwitzer, P. (1999). 'Implementation intentions: Strong effects of simple plans.' *American Psychologist*, 54(7), 493–503.

Hannibal, K.E. and Bishop, M.D. (2014). 'Chronic stress, cortisol dysfunction, and pain: A psychoneuroendocrine rationale for stress management in pain rehabilitation.' *Physical Therapy*, 94(12), 1816–1825.

Heijnen, S., Hommel, B., Kibele, A. and Colzato, L.S. (2016). 'Neuromodulation of aerobic exercise – a review.' *Frontiers in Psychology*, 6, 1890.

Herd, S., Mingus, B. and O'Reilly, R. (2010). 'Dopamine and self-directed learning.' *Frontiers in Artificial Intelligence and Applications*, 221, 58–63.

Jurado, M.-B. and Rosselli, M. (2007). 'The elusive nature of executive functions: A review of our current understanding.' *Neuropsychology Review*, 17(3), 213–233.

Kim, S.I. (2013). 'Neuroscientific model of motivational process.' *Frontiers in Psychology*, 4, 98.

Kok, P., Mostert, P. and de Lange, F. (2017). 'Prior expectations induce prestimulus sensory templates.' *Proceedings of the National Academy of Sciences*, 114(39), 10473–10478.

Koyama, T., McHaffie, J., Laurienti, P. and Coghill, R. (2005). 'The subjective experience of pain: Where expectations become reality.' *Proceedings of the National Academy of Sciences*, 102(36), 12950–12955.

Lewis, N. Jr and Oyserman, D. (2015). 'When does the future begin? Time metrics matter: Connecting present and future selves.' *Psychological Science*, 13, 219–224.

Miller, E. and Cohen, J. (2001). 'An integrative theory of prefrontal cortex function.' *Annual Review of Neuroscience*, 24(1), 167–202.

Pezzulo, G. and Castelfranchi, C. (2009). 'Intentional action: From anticipation to goal-directed behavior.' *Psychological Research*, 73, 437–440.

Puglisi-Allegra, S. and Ventura, R. (2012). 'Prefrontal/accumbal catecholamine system processes high motivational salience.' *Frontiers in Behavioral Neuroscience*, 6, Article 31.

Schultz, W. (2015). 'Neuronal reward and decision signals: From theories to data.' *Physiological Reviews*, 95(3), 853–951.

Wolpe, N., Nombela, C. and Rowe, J. (2015). 'Dopaminergic modulation of positive expectations for goal-directed action: Evidence from Parkinson's disease.' *Frontiers in Psychology*, 6, Article 1514.

Wood, W. and Neal, D. (2007). 'A new look at habits and the habit–goal interface.' *Psychological Review*, 114(4), 843–63.

Wunderlich, K., Smittenaar, P. and Dolan, R.J. (2012). 'Dopamine enhances model-based over model-free choice behavior.' *Neuron*, 75(3), 418–424.

Yin, H.H. and Knowlton, B.J. (2006). 'The role of the basal ganglia in habit formation.' *Nature Reviews Neuroscience*, 7(6), 464–476.

Blogs

Launch Circuit

Merzenich, M. (2013). 'How you can make your brain smarter every day.' *Forbes*, 6 August. Available from www.forbes.com/sites/nextavenue/2013/08/06/how-you-can-make-your-brain-smarter-every-day [Accessed 30 September 2020].

ACCEPT with Strategic Control Circuit

University of California – Los Angeles (2007). 'Putting feelings into words produces therapeutic effects in the brain.' *ScienceDaily*, 22 June. Available from www.sciencedaily.com/releases/2007/06/070622090727.htm [Accessed 30 September 2020].

ADOPT with Inspiring Resilience Circuit

Pontin, J. (2014). 'The importance of feelings: The neuroscientist Antonio Damasio explains how minds emerge from emotions and feelings.' *MIT Technology Review*, 17 June. Available from www.technologyreview.com/2014/06/17/172310/the-importance-of-feelings [Accessed 30 September 2020].

INDEX

D

E

F

M

N

T

ABOUT THE AUTHOR

Frederique Murphy is a leadership mindset strategist who inspires and equips leaders to move through extraordinary change. Her Mountain Moving Mindset (M3) platform delivers inspiration and scientific strategies, instilling beliefs, attitudes and behaviours to drive powerful transformations.

She brings together 17 years' experience in corporate change for large multinational organizations and scientific expertise in positive psychology, neuroscience and behaviour change with strategic vision and business acumen, having run her award-winning speaking, training and consulting company for the past decade. With this impactful combination, she helps organizations – including Fortune 500 companies – and associations reap the benefits of tapping into the power of their leaders' minds to rewire their brains for success and make change happen.

Frederique regularly writes for business publications, has been interviewed on national and international radio and podcast shows, and serves her large audience via her award-winning M3 blog and podcast *The M3 Mile*. She is powerful at connecting with people and loves engaging with her remarkable online community – her M3 Power Community spans all continents and includes over 155,000 leaders, with whom she shares her ever-growing mind and brain expertise.

When Frederique takes to the stage, sparks fly: she is a passionate and charismatic speaker who captivates audiences and awakens the neural paths in their brains. She has delivered her popular 'Lead Beyond The Edge' keynote to tens of thousands of professionals around the globe, from Dublin to Vancouver to Mexico to Amsterdam to Madrid to Dallas.

For more information on Frederique's transformational range, visit www.FrederiqueMurphy.com, join the free M3 Power Community and start climbing now!